Amateur Wine Making

Outdoor grapes in the author's vineyard

AMATEUR
WINE MAKING

*An Introduction and Complete Guide to
Wine, Cider, Perry, Mead and Beer Making
and to the Cultivation of the Vine*

by

S. M. TRITTON
M.P.S., F.R.I.C.

FABER AND FABER
3 Queen Square
London

First published in 1956
by Faber and Faber Limited
Second edition 1959
Reprinted 1961
Third edition 1964
Reprinted 1966
New and revised edition 1968
Reprinted 1970 and 1971
Printed in Great Britain by
Western Printing Services Limited, Bristol
All rights reserved

ISBN 0 571 04646 0

Contents

7

List of Tables

9

Illustrations

Introduction

There is at the present time a great and growing interest in wines and vines in this country. During the war years wine making was one of the many things which had perforce to be neglected and afterwards its revival was held back by sugar rationing and other shortages. Now that times are more propitious it is good to see this revival in the art of wine making and to find that the younger generation are not ignoring it although they did not know it in their youth. The aim of this book is not only to revive the skill or instil the art of wine making but also to explain the underlying principles in such a manner that the veriest amateur without scientific background can learn to understand what is happening during the various stages of the process. Certain technical terms may creep in but reference to a glossary of terms used in wine making on page 234 will soon assist the reader to understand and become familiar with the terminology used by vintners. It is furthermore hoped that this introduction to the art of wine making will not only help amateurs to become successful in their own efforts but also stimulate their interest in wines generally. Wine drinking is a habit which could well be encouraged in this country and there is no doubt the consumption of wine with meals tends to turn even the simplest meal into a festive occasion. Experience shows that the more the amateur experiments with his own wines and the more successful he is in producing them, the more he will purchase Continental wines both as a standard against which to compare his own and because of a developing taste for and a developing habit of wine drinking.

It is well within an amateur wine-maker's capacity to produce all the different types of wines desired for any social occasion both from grapes and the other fruits of the garden.

Those who are fortunate enough to possess a vine in a greenhouse or on a house wall or a number of vines growing in rows in the garden will find in this book the required knowledge to produce a variety of grape wines. As, in addition, very little authentic information is available on many aspects of grape growing, this will receive attention in the later portions of the book.

American readers please note:

| American pint | = 16 oz. |
| American gallon | = 128 oz. (i.e. 8 pints) |

| Imperial or British pint | = 20 oz. |
| Imperial gallon | = 160 oz. (i.e. 8 pints) |

When using American pints or gallons only $\frac{4}{5}$ of the amount of sugar or fruit given in the recipes should be used. It is not necessary to reduce the amounts of minor ingredients such as nutrient, grape tannin or acids.

Wine Types and a Brief Survey of the different Methods of Production

Wine—What is it?

Many people who drink wine do not consider the miracle which has been performed in turning a sometimes insipid fruit juice into a beverage which stimulates but does not inebriate, which has health-promoting properties, which turns a simple meal into a feast and which is a subject for appraisal by the simplest agricultural labourer and veriest of connoisseurs. The miracle of vinification (see glossary) rests entirely on the good offices of a most amazing and versatile organism which is termed yeast. Pasteur, a French chemist, was the first to elucidate the nature of yeast and published his researches in 1865 and from then to the present time continuous researches on yeast and yeast activity have been carried out in many countries. All the functions which yeast can perform are even now not completely understood but it has been established that wine making is only possible through the activity of yeasts. The yeast cell is rounded or egg shaped and so minute that it can only be seen through a powerful microscope; it requires millions of cells to turn a sugary fruit juice into an alcoholic beverage. Yeast is able to split up the sugar into a gas called carbon dioxide, which comes off in bubbles, and into alcohol which remains in the liquid. Gradually much or all of the sugar disappears and by this means a wine is produced. As yeast can only continue working in this way until a certain concentration of alcohol has been formed and as fruit juice may contain more sugar than the yeast can ferment or 'work', then the wines may remain sweet. Other fruit juices containing less sugar will lose all this sugar and become what is known as dry.

Making different Wine Types

It is within the vintner's or wine maker's capacity to make any type of wine. Either white or red, still or sparkling, sweet or dry, sherry-like, port-like, spiced like vermouth or flavoured, either by a distinctive fruit juice like that of muscat grape or raspberry, or with a flavour of the yeast as in the case of a Sauterne or a Tokay wine. It takes many years of experience to ensure the same result each time a wine is made but approximately similar wines can be obtained by using standard juices, a suitable yeast and by adhering to a similar procedure in making and maturing.

Wines for different occasions

The vintner may wish to know the range of wines which are suitable for different occasions. In general, sherries are drunk as *aperitives*, that is, as appetizers before a meal or at the start of a meal with soup, while dry white wine is served with fish or white meat and red wines with red meat; sweeter wines such as Sauterne or Barsac are drunk with the dessert while sweet fortified wines or liqueurs follow the meal. Champagne is served on festive occasions or with the dessert.

APERITIVE WINES

Production of Sherry

Sherry is a wine produced from white grapes in the South of Spain. The grapes are grown on poor chalky soil and the size of the crop is kept restricted so as to ensure that the juice will contain a high proportion of sugar. Only ripe grapes are gathered into baskets holding about 25 lb. of grapes and these are then transported by mule to the press house (see plate 1) where, to increase the sugar content, the grapes are emptied on to esparto grass mats and are exposed to the sun for twenty-four hours, being covered only at night (see plate 2).

When the grapes are dry and sun warmed they are emptied into a lagar where men wearing nail studded leather boots crush the grapes but avoid breaking the pips (see plate 4); the latter contain oil which would spoil the wine. The juice is allowed to run out into barrels through a funnel provided with a strainer. When most of the juice has run off, the pulp is heaped round the screw of a press and held in position by winding long lengths of 4" esparto grass bands round the pulp. A board which fits onto the screw is laid on top of the pulp and pressure applied by men screwing the board down on to the pulp. The juice which runs out is mixed with the juice obtained when the grapes were trodden. A further quantity of juice can be obtained by using hydraulic pressure but such juice is not used for the making of sherry but mainly for a wine which will be distilled to provide spirit for fortifying.

The casks, known as butts, are taken to the Bodega where the wine is looked after by highly experienced vintners (see plate 3).

Fermentation takes place very rapidly and is soon complete; at the first cold spell the wine starts to clear. It is then drained off the yeast deposit and blended into casks which are only filled seven-eighths full (see plate 5).

The wine will throw a second yeast deposit but will not be racked again; but part of the wine will be transferred from time to time and will be replaced by younger wine. During the whole process of blending and maturing sherries are exposed to air and after the first racking, that is drawing off from the yeast deposit, sherries remain on the yeast till they are drawn off for bottling or for sale in cask. As will be seen later, all other wines have to be protected from air as otherwise they will spoil. Sherries are deliberately exposed to air so as to produce an *oxidized* wine. (Oxidized means affected by the oxygen of the air.) The older and more oxidized sherries get the finer is their flavour and the darker the colour, with the exception of sherries which have grown a skin of wrinkled appearance known as a *Sherry Flor*. Such sherries are pale and dry and are called *finos*. The vintner cannot foresee which wine will become a fino or which wine will darken and in time become an *oloroso*. He therefore leaves the wine in a nursery called the *anada* till it becomes obvious in which way the wine will develop, after which it is transferred to the first *criadera* in a system of blending known as a *solera* where casks are stacked three or sometimes four high and where the bottom cask contains the oldest wine and the top cask the youngest. Sometimes two or three such stacks are used for the blending of one grade of sherry and the blend may go through as many as eleven stages, each of which is called a criadera until the last one, the final blend, which is termed the solera. By removing no more than one-fifth of the content of a butt at one time, transferring it to the next criadera and replacing it from an earlier criadera, the wine will tend to remain uniform (see plate 6).

Sherries are fortified to about 17 per cent of alcohol prior to maturing and further fortified when drawn off for shipment to between 20 per cent and 22 per cent. Dark sherries are generally sweetened with a grape concentrate and all sherries are fined with white of egg about one month before despatch. Because of its high alcohol content sherry is not drunk as freely as a table wine.

Vermouth

This aperitif can be either sweet with about 18 per cent of sugar or dry when the sugar content is about 4 per cent. It is produced from a white wine flavoured with Vermouth and a variety of other herbs, sweetened with cane sugar and brought up to about 18 per cent of alcohol by volume by the addition of 90 per cent alcohol. It is usual to use a wine with a neutral taste as any predominant flavour would conflict with that imparted by the herbs.

DINNER WINES

Dry White Wines

All dry wines of commerce are made from grape juice. For white wines the grapes (generally white but red grapes can be

1. Sherry grapes being transported by mule to the press house

2. Grapes being dried on esparto mats outside the press house prior
to Sherry making

3. A vineyard scene near Jerez. The grape juice departing to the Bodega

4. Treading the grapes in the lagar by men wearing special nail-studded leather boots which crush the grapes but not the pips

used) are crushed and the juice is pressed out by hand-operated or power presses.

The juice is run into barrels, which are only partially filled and fermentation is preferably brought about by adding a yeast starter which should have been prepared a few days before the harvest. When the fermentation, which will at first be vigorous, has quietened down, the cask is *filled right to the bung hole* and a fermentation lock (see p. 28) placed in position to protect the wine. The inquiring mind will wonder why the fermenting vessel is not filled up at once. The answer is that the wine at first produces so much foam that it would exude through the top of the cask. Filling the barrel full after the fermentation has quietened down and inserting a fermentation lock filled with water protects the wine from vinegar flies and from the oxidizing effect of the air. All wines, with the exception of sherries, can be spoilt if exposed unduly to the atmosphere. There is no danger of the wine being spoilt during the early vigorous fermentation as the gas which is evolved drives out all the air.

Dry Red Wines

These are of course made from red grapes, but unlike white wines the red wine has to be made from the whole grape berry. Only as fermentation proceeds will sufficient colour be extracted from the skins by the alcohol formed to give a richly coloured wine. Most grape juice, even in red grapes, is colourless; though there are some grapes with red juice, but this is too pale to give good colour to the wine. The grapes are put through a grape mill which will remove the stalks and break the berries, but not the pips. This pulp is then mixed with some yeast and the fermentation must be allowed to carry on till enough colour has been extracted. Anything from five to fourteen days may be required. The mass of grape skins will tend to form a solid layer on top of the open container where the fermentation is carried out. This mass is called a *cap* and it is very liable to turn to vinegar if it remains on top of the liquid as fruit flies may settle on it and introduce bacteria which cause the formation of vinegar. It is therefore usual to hold the cap down below the surface of the liquid by a perforated disc which allows the liquid to stream through the cap. As soon as the vigorous fermentation has subsided the wine below the cap is drawn off into casks which are immediately filled to the top and the fermentation allowed to continue in these casks.

DESSERT WINES

There are a number of different sweet wines which are usually drunk with the sweet or fruit course. Those best known are the Sauternes and Barsacs, which are produced in the Bordeaux district of France, while Tokay is a similar sweet wine made in Hungary. Finely flavoured sweet wines are also produced occasionally in the colder parts of the Continent as, for instance, the Rhine and Mosel district of Germany, in years when the weather has been particularly favourable with high autumn temperatures which induce berries to dry out whilst still on the vine. Wine from such raisinified berries is called *Trockenbeere* wine, while if berries are actually selected by hand the wines produced from their juice are called *Ausleese* wines and are always of superb flavour. Wines are also made from grapes which have grown a mould called the '*noble mould*' and it is one of the strangest things in the history of wine making that the first Sauternes were made more or less by accident. During a vintage in a year in which the grapes had gone mouldy the vintner in desperation decided to press them and found much to his surprise that a very fine wine resulted. Most sweet wines are made from over-ripe grapes or even in many cases from mouldy grapes. Care must be exercised though that only grapes which *were really ripe and then have gone mouldy* are used to make a sweet wine. In that case this mould will make the grape juice still sweeter and bring about other changes which will result in sweet wines with a very fine flavour. This is the reason for calling it the *noble mould*, but it is not possible to make such wines from unripe grapes which have gone mouldy. Dessert wines can stand a little more air than dry table wines and may take two or three years to mature.

SPARKLING WINES

Champagne

This famous wine is usually rendered sparkling by renewed fermentation in bottle whereby the gas is retained. Such a wine was first developed in the Champagne district of France but sparkling wines are produced in other countries, notably Germany. Champagne is produced from a dry wine generally made from the juice of red grapes in the autumn and left to clear during the winter. Then it is tested and the necessary amounts of sugar, a yeast nutrient and a champagne yeast are added. This mixture is bottled and the wine is allowed to referment in the bottle. The bottles are particularly strong and the corks are wired in. The bottles are laid on their sides in a cold cellar for four to five years and when the fermentation has ceased the bottles are placed into a board provided with oval holes. Here the bottles are twisted at frequent intervals to shake the yeast down on to the cork and gradually the bottles are brought from an angle of forty-five degrees to the vertical. When the neck of the bottle faces downwards it is inserted in a freezing mixture to freeze about one inch of the wine containing all the yeast deposit. The bottle is then turned right side up, the wire is cut and the pressure within the bottle will make the cork and the adherent plug of ice fly out. The inside of the neck is quickly wiped by the little finger and the bottle is at once filled with some sweetened grape spirit and a new cork inserted and wired down.

Carbonated Wines

These have recently been developed in Germany, and are known as Perlwein. They are made from dry or slightly sweet white wine, rendered effervescent by carbonating with the gas carbon dioxide in the same way as the effervescent fruit drinks marketed in this country. Such a process requires special costly machinery and is therefore not suitable for amateurs.

AFTER DINNER WINES

After dinner wines are all fortified wines. They include Madeira, Marsala, Malaga, Tarragona, and Port. Madeira comes from the Island of Madeira and is made from white grapes. The fortified wines of Madeira are all brown which is partly due to heating the young wine before fortifying, partly to the action of air and partly to the incorporation of some grape concentrate for sweetening. The darkening of the wine is termed *maderisation* and this term is now applied to any wine which yellows or browns on maturing.

Marsala which is somewhat similar to Madeira, is the product of white grapes which are grown in Sicily and is exported from the port of Marsala.

Malaga comes from Southern Spain and is produced mainly from the Pedro Ximenez grapes. These are reputed to be a type of Riesling grape given to Spain by Peter Siemens, the Spanish version of his name becoming Pedro Ximenez. It is an exceedingly attractive rich and sweet fortified wine.

Tarragona is situated on the East coast of Spain. Its wines aim to be somewhat like port but although sweet and pleasant they lack the quality of a port wine.

Port is frequently called the Englishman's wine. It certainly was that during those days of gracious living and sufficient domestic help when the family could linger over their port and cheese and then when the ladies retired to the drawing room for coffee the men passed round the decanter, always to the left. Having recently visited Oporto and having had the chance to stay with the shippers of Dow's Port it was wonderful to experience for a while the felicity of this gracious living. Servants are good and plentiful and all household chores are performed by them. Even the simplest houses have resident domestic help and this does allow for greater leisure and for the consumption of after-dinner wines. The history of Port is very interesting. Originally it was not fortified but a sweet red wine. When a visitor to the country decided to ship some to England it was thought advisable to make the wine more stable by the addition of grape spirit.

This was found to be such an improvement that the technique of Port wine production was completely altered. Instead of adding grape spirit to the finished wine, grape spirit was added to stop the fermentation while the juice was still sweet and this stopped yeast activity for a while. When the yeast again started working new additions of grape spirit prevented further fermentation. The grapes used for Port are red but gradually the wine loses the red colour and becomes tawny. Many different types of wines are produced in Portugal but only a limited area is allowed to grow vines for the making of Port. This area is called the Douro and consists of steep valleys at both sides of the upper reaches of the River Douro which enters the sea at Oporto, which means The Port (see plates 7 and 9). The vines are kept quite short and pruning is severe even in this southern climate. The grapes are trodden in lagars similar to the Spanish lagars but with deeper sides. The treading is done by two rows of men with bare feet who pass across the lagar in closed ranks till they meet in the middle (see plate 10). This treading continues for four hours on end and after a rest is resumed till sufficient colour has been extracted from the skins. The pulp is then pressed and the juice allowed to ferment to a certain degree after which it is fortified and sent down to the Wine Lodges at Oporto. Here the wine is blended, treated, stored and prepared for shipment (see plate 8). There are several varieties of Ports, Red, Tawny, White and Vintage. The last named are produced in a year when the vintage is particularly good,

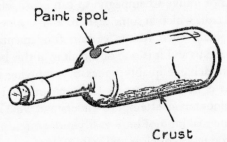

Paint spot

Crust

To prevent the crust from being disturbed through inadvertently turning the bottle, each is marked by a spot of paint on the top

are not shipped till at least two years old and are then bottled on arrival and stored for years on their sides to allow the wine to mature and to throw a crust. Such bottles are marked with a spot of paint on the side which is uppermost so that the wine can be decanted without disturbing the crust. The wine is shipped to England in casks called *pipes* which contain 115–118 gallons.

FRUIT WINES

All the wines discussed above are made from grapes. Wines can also be made from other fruits but by an order called the 'Labelling Order' they must be labelled by the appropriate prefix to the word wine, for instance, blackberry wine, apple wine, etc. That is, no wine may be called just wine unless it is made from grapes. If wine is made from fruits with distinctive flavours such as raspberry, plum, blackberry, gooseberry, then they tend to retain a fruity flavour till they have had a considerable period of ageing. On the other hand fruits with a less predominant flavour such as apple, pear, rhubarb, and red and white currant can readily be made to simulate wines from grapes. When visiting the Champagne district I was given to understand that at one time rhubarb wine was imported from Norfolk into France to blend with the local white wine which was to be converted into champagne. This shows that rhubarb wine can be as good as a white wine and just as it is possible to make from apples a Champagne Cider that is not unlike Champagne so can other wines be made from English fruit which in some cases resemble wines made from grapes. To obtain such results certain fundamental principles must be adhered to and it is one of the aims of this book to assist the amateur to achieve quality wines by supplying the required knowledge. It is not necessary to know chemistry to be able to make good wines but an attempt to understand what is happening will make wine making not only vastly more interesting but also lead to the production of clear and stable wines.

𝟤

Theoretical Aspects of Wine Production

Wine made from Grapes

There are two schools of thought on wine making. One considers that good wine can be made by simply following recipes while the other stresses the need for understanding the simple underlying principles of wine making. Admittedly the wines of commerce have been made successfully for centuries but only as the result of long experience. Furthermore making wines from grapes is far easier than from other fruit, because the grape juice contains all the necessary ingredients and mostly in the right proportions for wine making. To prepare any type of wine sound principles of vinification must be followed to ensure a sound product. A consideration of the reasons why making grape wine is easier than making fruit wine may help the wine maker to understand some of the underlying principles.

The constituents of grape juice or must

Grape juice which is to be fermented into wine is properly called *must*. This contains all the ingredients required for a satisfactory end product, namely wine. First of all sugar has to be present. Normal grape juice, or must, contains the right amount of sugar in good years but in bad years a little may have to be added. The important thing is that there is not normally TOO MUCH sugar present. Yeasts cannot ferment excess of sugar and many wine makers court disaster by adding too much sugar at the start of fermentation. Also the must will contain sufficient nitrogenous matter to nourish the yeast and produce a good yeast crop. Yeasts are normally present on the fruit and can produce a fermentation *but* these yeasts are accompanied by many disease-producing organisms such as vinegar bacteria and other bacteria which may produce bad butterlike flavours. So even for grape wines pure yeast cultures are used at the start of the season to ensure good quality wines. Last but not least grape juice contains sufficient acid to prevent bacterial spoilage of the wine. Unless fruit acids like tartaric or citric are present wines will tend to have a medicine-like flavour.

PRINCIPLES OF VINIFICATION FOR THE PRODUCTION OF SOUND WINES

The use of sulphite

One of the most important factors in producing good wines is the use of sulphurous acid or a compound of sulphurous acid called *sodium* or *potassium metabisulphite* (note not sul*phide* as mentioned in some wine books. The sulphide smells of bad eggs, and would completely spoil a wine). Some purists hold that the use of chemicals in wine is quite indefensible but this is of course nonsense as chemicals, in one form or another, have always been used in wine making. From medieval times sulphur was burnt in the barrels and thus converted into sulphurous acid gas and this is still frequently done nowadays. The barrels were then filled with the juice to be fermented and again the finished wine was put into barrels which had been treated by burning sulphur. As sulphur burns it is converted into sulphur dioxide which dissolves in water to form *sulphurous acid* (please note not sulph*uric* acid). This gas is similar to a sulphite except that it is a gas and is absorbed by the juice or wine as it flows into the barrel. By such primitive methods it is not possible to judge the amount of sulphite in the juice or the wine and so it can easily be overdone. By using a solid salt of *sulphurous acid*, namely *potassium* or *sodium metabisulphite*, it is possible to ensure that an exact and known amount is present. It is most convenient for amateurs to use this salt as compressed tablets and as such it is sold in the form of *Campden Tablets*. Each Campden Tablet contains 7 grains (0·44 grams) of metabisulphite and one tablet added to a gallon gives a solution containing 50 parts per million of sulphur dioxide. The use of these tablets will be discussed further under 'The Practice of Wine Making'.

Browning and its prevention

One of the most important rules in winemaking is to protect the wine at all stages from air; otherwise it will go brown and develop off flavours, even if it does not go to vinegar. Hence barrels must be topped up, kept bung full and where possible stored with the bung at the side; bottles must be kept on their sides so that no air can get into them through the corks becoming dry as they would in an upright bottle. But more than just protection from air is needed; this is why sulphite is added as it has several beneficial effects, including the power to prevent oxidation of the wine. Hence it is called an *anti-oxidant*. On the other hand great care has to be exercised to avoid too much sulphite being added since it can impart a wholly undesirable flavour to the wine.

Normally it is sufficient to add one Campden tablet per gallon (which corresponds to 50 parts per million) to the must prior to fermentation to kill undesirable bacteria and to reduce the effects of wild yeasts; but if the fruit was at all mouldy then two should be used.

After fermentation, but not until the second racking, more sulphite should be added to prevent browning; for table wines, both dry and sweet, ½ to 1 tablet is desirable but wines vary in their tendency to browning so sometimes more proves necessary. The amount required can be found by a simple test which will be described under 'The Practice of Wine Making' (page 91) but the quantity added should preferably not exceed a total of 3 tablets per gallon as otherwise a sulphite flavour may be noticeable. However it is possible that this amount of sulphite may be barely sufficient to prevent oxidation or browning so one or two Reductone Tablets per gallon are recommended because these are also an effective anti-oxidant but are tasteless and entirely wholesome, that is they cannot adversely affect the quality of the wine.

Sherries, Madeiras and Ports are not sulphited as these wines are improved by taking up oxygen and browning.

Use of the Fermentation Lock

During the vigorous fermentation, also called the primary fermentation, a layer of the gas which is evolved will prevent air getting at the liquid because the gas is heavier than air and so lies on the surface. But in addition a *fermentation lock* or *trap* must be inserted to prevent vinegar flies getting at the wine (see also pages 19 and 50).

The process of racking

Wine would be entirely lacking in vinosity and would develop off flavours if it were not periodically removed from its deposit. This is invariably done by vintners and is termed *racking*, the wine being drawn off through the barrel tap from the *lees*, as the residue is called. These lees contain a lot of impurities as well as much yeast. The wine, which has then been transferred to another clean barrel will have to be topped up with some spare wine to ensure the barrel being full. After three or four months the wine is racked again and so on at three- to four-monthly intervals. Some sulphite may have to be added at racking time to ensure that the wine keeps in sound condition while maturing.

Pulp fermentation and cap formation

Any wine which is made by fermenting in the presence of pulp is liable to spoilage. As mentioned under red wine production the solid portions will float up to form a *cap* which is a wonderful breeding ground for vinegar flies and bacteria. The fermenting vessel must be kept covered and the cap has either to be pushed down several times during the day to allow colour to be extracted or held down by a perforated board called a *sinker*. Many fruit wines are also made by fermenting on the pulp for shorter or longer periods. This is done to confer both colour and body on the wine but care must be taken not to leave the pulp in the wine longer than necessary as this may lead to wines which will not clarify and may taste astringent or bitter.

Principles of fruit wine production

Fruit wines, like wines made from grapes, fall into two main classes, i.e. red and white wines. Also the same five different types can be made: dry dinner wines, both red and white, sparkling wines, sweet dessert wines, after-dinner fortified wines and aperitive wines like sherry and vermouth.

It may be thought that the fruit flavour of some English fruit will persist and so prevent sauterne or sherry-like flavours being obtained and to a certain extent this is true in young wines, but by proper procedure and suitable ageing wines closely approaching the wines of commerce can be produced.

All fruit juices, except dried fruit and, of course, good quality grapes, lack sugar and it is important that the *right amount* of cane sugar is added. Over sugaring leads to failure. It is better to add too little at first and then to feed with more sugar *dissolved in fruit juice or water* than to hope for a strong wine by adding too much sugar at the start. Feeding with sugar leads to the production of strong wines as the yeast does not have to ferment too much sugar to start with, but the sugar should always be dissolved in some of the wine or in water for if added as a solid it may easily stay at the bottom of the vessel and then spoil the yeast. Directions on the use of sugar or syrup will be given in 'The Practice of Wine Making', pages 43 seqq.

Also some fruit juices are so sour that water has to be added to reduce the acidity by dilution, as in the case of the juice of red or white currants, while other juices lack acid which must be added; the best acid to use is *citric acid*. When water is added this must be taken into account in deciding on the amount of sugar required.

Yeast Nutrient

When making fruit wines it is important to realize that, partly because it is necessary to add water or syrup or even sugar, each of which occupies space and increases the volume, the yeast nutrients in the juice tend to be diluted and so may be insufficient for a sound fermentation. Grapes contain more nitrogenous matter than other fruits. These natural nutrients are essential for adequate yeast growth but the addition of an ammonium salt obtainable as a ready prepared *yeast nutrient* is essential when natural yeast nutrients are low, and is always advocated for fruit wines. Yeast cannot grow properly in a sugar solution only, even with the addition of a yeast nutrient. Failing the proteins present in fruit juices, malt extract or a cereal should be added, as these contain the requisite proteins (see also page 74).

The uses and properties of yeast

Having shown that the fruit juice which is to be fermented should be properly adjusted by the addition where necessary of sugar, acid and yeast nutrient and, of course, yeast, the function of the yeast and the choice of a suitable yeast must now be discussed. First of all the wine maker will desire to know how yeast originates. Actually, yeasts are always present in the bloom on the surface of various fruits but these are not all pure wine yeasts but a mixture of various yeasts including those which do not form much alcohol. There are some yeasts which produce bad flavours and others, by tending to break down rather easily, make a wine muddy coloured and unstable. In addition, these natural yeasts are often heavily contaminated with moulds and vinegar bacteria which are obviously undesirable, hence the importance of adding a pure culture of yeast and the choice of a suitable wine yeast cannot be over-emphasized. There are available a variety of wine yeasts but for general wine making a good sedimentary yeast is all that is necessary, unless it is desired to make wines like champagne, sherry or port.

Yeast and wine quality

When introducing wine yeast into fruit juice it may take quite a while before fermentation is noted. Actually the yeast must first multiply sufficiently and it requires many millions of yeast cells to ferment a wine. Yeasts grow by budding and each yeast, which in the case of wine yeast is generally egg shaped, is able to grow young yeasts. It does this by pushing out a minute bud which will split off from the mother cell when it has grown large enough. A yeast can bud about thirty times before it becomes exhausted and it is quite easy to see, therefore, why yeasts grow so very quickly. One cell will produce 30 new yeasts, 30 will produce 900 and 900 will produce 810,000 and so on. It takes about $2\frac{1}{2}$ hours for a yeast to become fully grown, and in about 4 hours the quantity of yeast will have doubled. It is only when there are sufficient yeasts present that fermentation will be obvious and in the first instance the fruit juice will become charged with gas. When this starts to come away from the liquid by pushing through the fermentation lock a certain amount of foam will also be noticed. On the other hand, fermentation is sometimes very slow, either because the liquid is too cold or it contains too much sugar or not enough yeast food. Also, if only a little sugar is present the fermentation will finish quite quickly due to the yeast having used up the available sugar so that no more gas formation is possible.

The disadvantage of baker's yeast

At one time the only yeasts available to amateur wine makers in this country were brewer's and baker's yeasts. Neither of these yeasts is likely to give good flavours nor do they produce wines with vinosity or which are clear and stable. Baker's yeast also has the disadvantage that the wine made with it is frequently cloudy and covered by a film. Moreover this yeast does not settle to form a firm layer such as is the case with a sedimentary wine yeast. This means that such wines cannot be drawn off without disturbing the yeast which will float up. Furthermore in old-fashioned recipes far too great a quantity of yeast is advocated with the result that a bubbling vigorous fermentation ensues. This is highly undesirable. For wine making the fermentation should be as slow and steady as possible. The bubbling fermentation is wanted when making beer and so larger quantities of yeasts can be added, but even there it is not necessary. When fermentation is very slow it is sometimes only noticed by a ring of bubbles round the perimeter of the liquid, that is, at the surface between the container and the edge of the liquid. Those wine makers who are used to baker's yeast will be surprised at the quietness of a normal vinous fermentation but the slower and the more steady the fermentation the better will the quality of the wine be. Even wine yeasts can vary in the flavour they confer on a wine. There are some champagne yeasts which confer a straw-like taste on the wine, while others give much better flavours; hence the fact that a yeast is called a champagne yeast is no guarantee that it will produce a sparkling wine of a desired flavour. It is therefore important to use yeasts which have been tested for their flavour-producing capacity.

Selected varieties of wine yeasts

Special wine yeasts which have undergone such tests are now available and have proved very successful in giving much better wines than hitherto. The range is quite extensive but for most purposes the *All Purpose Sedimentary Wine Yeast* gives entirely satisfactory results. On the other hand, for Champagne making a Champagne yeast is needed as this yeast will not stick to the bottom of the container or bottle and so can be removed by the methods employed during Champagne production. To obtain Port wine or Sherry flavours the respective yeasts are preferable. Many wine makers experiment with the entire range of yeasts as without doubt they all confer different flavours on the wines.

Details of how to use the yeasts are given in the practical section. It suffices here to mention that the yeasts which are available[1]

[1] Obtainable from Grey Owl Laboratories Ltd., Kingswood, Bristol.

are either grown on a wedge-shaped piece of a jelly-like substance called agar in a tube or in a bottle as a liquid yeast. By suitable means the yeasts are propagated further and the yeast from a tube can be increased first by making a starter and increasing this by stages to ferment any quantity of wine. On the other hand liquid cultures are now so cheap and so easy to use that most winemakers now use either half or the whole contents of a bottle for each batch of wine. It is possible to keep the yeast alive in a starter bottle during the whole season of wine making but it is desirable to use a fresh culture each year at the start of the wine-making season.

Yeast and alcoholic fermentation

When yeast has multiplied sufficiently and taken up a considerable amount of the available yeast food from the juice it will start to convert the sugar into carbon dioxide and alcohol; this process is called fermentation. For the purpose of calculation it will be sufficient to reckon that two parts of sugar will give you one part of alcohol, and one part of carbon dioxide. Starting therefore with a liquid containing 20 per cent of sugar, which is a very usual figure for grape juice, a wine with 10 per cent of alcohol will be produced. These figures are only approximate (see also page 40) and are given to explain the relationship between sugar content and alcohol in the wine. Generally the wine maker refers to tables to help him in adjusting the juice before fermentation and so to enable him to produce the type of wine required. (Tables III and VIII.) A lot of nonsense is talked about the ability of yeasts to form a certain amount of alcohol. In some grape juices which have been obtained in very hot years when the berries will usually tend to raisinify on the stalk, there will be much sugar in the juice but the resulting wine will nevertheless be low in alcohol. This is entirely due to the fact that through over-ripening the juice will become low in yeast nutrient. Hence, less yeast is formed and it has to do more work than it can manage. Furthermore the high sugar content will weaken the yeast so that it cannot work efficiently. Therefore such wines remain excessively sweet and are low in alcohol. If the wines are not racked, the yeasts will put some of their own substance back into the wine by disintegrating (this is called *autolysis*) and then some renewed fermentation takes place and a little more alcohol is formed. Gradually over the years, sometimes two years are required, such wines become stronger and more and more flavoured through the breakdown of the yeast, the main flavour being entirely due to the yeast. This again shows the importance of using a wine yeast known to have a good flavour rather than a baker's yeast. On the other hand if the same yeast ferments a juice containing ample and preferably added yeast nutrient and a lesser proportion of sugar then all of this sugar is converted to alcohol. Wine yeast can easily produce 15 per cent of alcohol without any effort and when syrup is added subsequently up to 20 per cent and even 22 per cent of alcohol can be produced so that it is possible to make wines as strong as sherries without fortifying.

When yeasts are lacking in nourishment they produce particularly good flavours and wines made from musts which are not particularly lacking in nutrients nor are of natural high sugar content can be improved by racking before the primary fermentation has completed. This causes new yeasts to grow which use up all the available nutrients so that eventually some will die for lack of food and fermentation will cease with the wine retaining some residual sugar. Furthermore it is possible to vary the type of wine obtained by adjusting the gravity; for dry wine it is usual to start with a gravity between 80 and 100, while for a sweet wine a gravity between 130 to 150 is preferable. The importance and the significance of these figures will be discussed in the practical details on wine making, but it suffices to state here that the best dry wines of commerce are kept a little low in alcohol, about 10 per cent by volume is preferred, while for sweet wines the alcohol content will be about 15 per cent and for fortified wines it may go up to as much as 22 per cent.

5. Blending the young Sherry in casks

6. Sherries maturing in Soleras in a Spanish Bodega

Silva & Cosens, Dow's Port, Oporto

7. A vineyard in the Douro Valley

Silva & Cosens, Dow's Port, Oporto

8. A Wine Lodge in Oporto

Racking and yeast growth

In addition to fermenting the juice the choice of yeast affects other stages in wine production. During the fermentation the sugar will be used up and the gravity will drop and gradually the yeast will begin to settle. As the yeasts settle a certain amount of clarification takes place and when they have formed a reasonably firm deposit and the wine is fairly clear it is time to rack the wine. After each racking some more yeast will start to grow by budding and in doing so will again use up any available yeast food present and thus help to clarify and stabilize the wine. Yeasts which do not settle are called powder yeasts. These tend to make racking of wine difficult and to clog any filter used; they also tend to early autolysis, thus making a wine unstable. Although these yeasts give good flavours they should only be used for wines which are to be fortified, such as Port, Madeira or Malaga.

Fermentation stages

Wine makers often wonder how to decide when the primary fermentation, which is the first vigorous fermentation, ceases and the secondary starts. There is no very firm dividing line between the two stages.

Primary fermentation

The first or primary fermentation is very vigorous and its speed can be assessed by observing the evolution of gas which bubbles through the water in the fermentation lock. The more vigorous the fermentation the more rapidly will the gas bubble through the water.

Secondary fermentation

When the wine is nearly dry or has reached a fairly high alcohol content a slower fermentation ensues. This is called the secondary fermentation. The gravity will drop more rapidly during the primary fermentation than during secondary fermentation. This will be demonstrated by figures in the practical section.

Sticking fermentation

Sometimes a fermentation ceases prematurely and this state of arrested fermentation is called *sticking*. It is not always easy to determine the reason why it has occurred. The most common causes are over-sugaring, under-nourishment of the yeast, or fermenting at too high a temperature. Premature racking, that is removal of the yeast deposit before the fermentation has been completed, may bring about some sticking. Lack of sufficient yeast food, such as the proteins and albumins normally present in fruit and vegetables, may result in insufficient yeast to complete the fermentation. Futhermore, some fruits such as bilberries or any fruit which has been dried or canned will be lacking in the vitamins needed for satisfactory yeast growth. In the latter case a Vitamin Yeast Energizer[1] is needed, *while for the former the addition of a yeast nutrient is desirable*. Yeast may also become exhausted through lack of air and stirring air into the vessel or pouring the wine from one vessel to another sometimes proves a remedy. Sometimes sticking is due to the cold weather and fermentation may be encouraged to start again by bringing the wine into a warm place. Failing that, or if the addition of yeast food has no effect, then some fresh yeast brew may have to be added. After sticking renewed fermentation is a frequent occurrence and at this stage the wine will frequently become bright and exhibit improved flavours.

Bottle fermentation

This fermentation after bottling is also called secondary fermentation. Actually it would be better to call it tertiary fermentation as wines should never be bottled till the secondary fermentation is complete, and bottle fermentation should not occur if the wine has been racked sufficiently.

[1] Grey Owl Laboratories Ltd., Almondsbury, nr. Bristol.

Stabilization of wines

Some vintners try to prevent fermentation after bottling by adding large quantities of sulphite but this is not a true remedy. The *only* way to prevent bottle fermentation is to rack the wines at regular intervals for a number of times or to employ sterile filtration. The latter process cannot be conducted by amateurs as it requires special plant; on the other hand, filtration through suitable fine grain filter paper is a partial safeguard but tends to be very slow. Filtration through asbestos pulp is much quicker and wines filtered through asbestos are frequently quite stable. Incidentally, this means that the wine will undergo rather prolonged exposure to the air which may spoil the colour and flavour but there are means of preventing this spoilage such as treatment with Campden tablets. Wine will always take up air when being racked—but actually a *little* air helps to mature the wine but it must not be overdone. Generally wines take up sufficient air during the first racking.

The influence of racking on stabilization

The effect of racking on wine quality must now be discussed. It will help to clarify and stabilize a wine and is quite simple to accomplish. When and how to rack will be more fully discussed under the 'Practice of Wine Making'. After racking and storing for one, two, or three months a new yeast crop will usually grow and form a deposit. This is invariably a very pure yeast with good fermentative power and can be used to make fresh yeast starters as required. During the time that new yeast deposit is forming the wine will become charged with carbon dioxide gas and when tasted will give a pricking sensation. After a while the yeast will start to ferment again and if the wine were left on its yeast deposit it would grow stronger, but frequently this is undesirable. Hence, wines must be racked at regular intervals to prevent renewed fermentation. Many wines are more attractive if the alcohol content is not too high and this is particularly the case in table wines.

Fining

This is a process frequently carried out during wine making but if wines are properly produced with sufficient wine yeast then fining should be unnecessary. Fining consists of adding a substance such as isinglass, white of egg, casein, agar or even milk to a wine. Gelatin is also used but only when tannin has been added prior to fining or for wines which are naturally high in tannin, as some rough red wines. A few drops of milk will fine a wine as the acid of the wine will curdle the milk which will settle down in floccules and pull hazy matter down with it. Yeast is also a good finer and stirring up the yeast deposit will often clear a wine. Some fruit wines are difficult to clear but this is frequently due to fermenting for too long on the pulp or to having too little yeast present due to lack of yeast nutrient. The clarification of wines by fining will be discussed further in the practical section on page 88 where a commercial fining is recommended.

The alcohol content of different wines

As mentioned earlier, there are different wine types and the difference is to a certain extent due to their alcohol content.

Aperitive and after dinner wines contain between 18 per cent and 22 per cent by volume.

Sweet dessert wines from 13 per cent to 15 per cent by volume.

Dry table wines range from 9 per cent to 12 per cent by volume.

It is quite easy to adjust a fruit juice to give a wine in the light dinner-wine class or the sweet dessert-wine range but for anything above 15 per cent of alcohol by volume the addition of grape spirit such as brandy or vodka may be required. Some fruit wines, notably plum, ferment without trouble to about 18 per cent to 20 per cent of alcohol by volume or sometimes even more.

Testing the gravity of juices and determination of the sugar content by the use of a hydrometer

The amount of alcohol which will be produced depends on the amount of sugar present in the juice. It is quite easy to determine the amount of sugar present by testing the gravity *prior to fermentation* and then referring to gravity tables which indicate the percentage of sugar present. Gravity determinations are quite simple to carry out by the use of an instrument called a hydrometer. These are not expensive and either one ranging from 1·000 to 1·300 or two are required, one of which ranges from 1·000 to 1·100 and the other from 1·100 to 1·200. These two cover the entire range of gravities which are normal in wine making. The use of the hydrometer will be explained in the practical section, but the theory of the gravity of liquids is not difficult to understand and is explained here.

Theory of specific gravity

Gravity is only another word for weight. The well-known schoolboy riddle: 'Which is heavier, a pound of feathers or a pound of lead?' gives the clue to the meaning of the word *Gravity*. A pound is a pound neither more nor less whether it is made up of feathers or lead. A pound of feathers will occupy quite a space while a pound of lead has only a very small bulk. It is obvious therefore that feathers weigh light and lead weighs heavy, or in other words lead has a high gravity.

Relationship between specific gravity and gravity

Sometimes gravity is spoken of as specific gravity and that means a gravity as compared to a specific substance, in fact a standard. The standard chosen is water and its specific gravity is recorded as 1·000. If a juice has a specific gravity of 1·085 this can also be spoken of as a gravity of 85, or a specific gravity of 1·160 is called a gravity of 160. In other words the figure 1 in front of the point and the nought immediately behind it are ignored. Where a specific gravity is less than 1·000 this cannot be expressed as gravity but only as specific gravity, i.e. 0·985.

Dissolved solids the cause of gravity

Now, what causes this gravity? If anything solid is dissolved in water then the gravity goes up. Fruit juice is only water in which there are dissolved sugar, acids, organic soluble matter suitable for yeast growth, colouring matter and tannin. All these make the water heavier and the higher the sugar content the higher the gravity. Grape juice may have gravities ranging from round about 60 to 120 or 160 but if the grape berries are partially dried out gravity may even exceed 200.

Relationship between sugar content and gravity

As the percentage of sugar increases in a juice or a syrup so the gravity increases. The sugar will be used up during the fermentation and this will then cause the gravity to drop. Firstly because less sugar is there, but also because the alcohol formed weighs much less than water and the gravity decreases still further through the presence of the alcohol.

Relationship between the gravity of a fruit juice and the alcohol content after fermentation

It is possible to determine the percentage of alcohol which may be expected by determining the gravity of the juice and looking up a table which gives this relationship or which shows the gravity of sugar solutions and the corresponding sugar content. From the percentage of sugar it is possible to calculate the approximate alcohol content. For two reasons figures which are given in different text-books do not always agree as to the amount of alcohol which may be expected. One is that the yeast uses up some sugar for growth and the second is that when the fermentation heats up there are sometimes considerable losses of alcohol. Generally speaking though, 100 gms. of sugar give 46 gms. of alcohol: or, by multiplying the weight of sugar by 0·46 the amount of alcohol by weight which should result is obtained. This has to be multiplied by 1·25 (approximately) to give the result in terms of the alcohol by volume or one can arrive at the volume of alcohol by multiplying the weight of sugar used by the factor 0·57. Another rough guide to the alcohol that may be expected is to use the gravity figure and divide this by 10 to give the alcohol by weight. An example will explain this: a gravity of $85 \div 10 =$ 8·5 per cent alcohol by weight,

or $8·5 \times 1\frac{1}{4} = 10·6$ per cent alcohol by volume.

Tables supplied by different authorities on wine making may indicate somewhat better alcohol yields amounting in the above case to 11·7 per cent; therefore the use of the gravity figure as suggested above is only a very rough approximation. Reference to a suitable sugar-alcohol table is more accurate, but it is useful to be able to calculate approximate results as given in the above examples.

From the foregoing it is clear that wines cannot be made entirely by a recipe. The wine maker cannot rely on precise instructions without himself or herself carrying out some simple tests. It is obvious that the same sugar addition to, say, an apple juice obtained from a cooking apple low in sugar will produce a juice containing less sugar and consequently have a lower gravity than if a sweet apple had been used to prepare the juice. If the wine maker cannot be bothered to test his juice for gravity then the only safe method is to add a minimum amount of sugar when starting the wine and increase the sugar content gradually.

Mistakes in wine recipes

In old-fashioned methods of wine making the use of bakers yeast is always suggested. Generally the addition of an ounce or so is advocated and the yeast is spread on toast and allowed to brew the wine. Such fermentation will be extremely vigorous and frequently will work itself out prematurely and only a weak wine low in alcohol will result. Furthermore, bottling is also frequently advocated *long* before the wine has had a chance to become stable and mature. Recipes for flower and root wines, and vegetable wines are frequently faulty because no acid or insufficient acid is advocated. This can cause the development of a medicine-like flavour.

Adjusting fruit juices for quality production

It cannot be over-emphasized that the wine maker must learn to use his judgment when preparing the juice for fermentation. He must adjust to a suitable gravity and acidity. If no acid is present, such as in parsnip or wines made from flowers $\frac{1}{2}$ per cent of citric acid must be added. $\frac{1}{2}$ per cent is equivalent to $\frac{1}{2}$ lb in 10 gallons or just under 1 oz. in 1 gallon. If too much acid is present as in white or red currants then some water must be added or some of the acid removed. Sometimes if a finished wine is much too sour, then it can be blended with a rather insipid and sweet wine. Sometimes astringency is lacking. Then this can be supplied by adding *grape tannin* or some pear peelings or oak leaves or strong tea. Guidance on such necessary adjustment will be given in the practical section but it must be emphasized that with an understanding of the principles involved and the exercise of a certain amount of judgment, better wines will be produced and thus will stimulate the art of wine making and consequently of wine drinking.

ℰ 3 ℨ

The Practice of Wine Making

WINE MAKING EQUIPMENT

Wine making does not require expensive apparatus and much of it can be made quite cheaply at home. Space is of course necessary if a variety of wines are to be produced but a few gallons or so can well be prepared in a kitchen or an outhouse while both garage and greenhouse can serve for storing and fermenting wine under cold or warm conditions.

Glass vessels, barrels and casks

It is desirable to have available different-size containers and 1 gallon glass jars, 4½ gallon barrels called a pin, 10 gallon glass carboys, 10 or 12 gallon casks and those exceeding this size are all useful for fermenting and for storage. Casks should be provided with a tap for drawing off and the fermentation should be carried out in barrels lying on their sides rather than standing up on end, as in plate 11.

The reason for this is that the flat end piece will dry out and much air will get into the wine due to the large exposed surface at the flat end. If the barrels lie on their sides and are kept full the surface of the liquid exposed to the air will be quite small and the staves of the barrel which are covered nearly to the bung hole will be kept wet by the wine and so will not tend to shrink. Whether barrels or glass jars are used a fermentation lock must be inserted.

Taps or Spiggots

Barrels must be provided with a suitable tap, also called a spiggot, but many wine makers do not insert a tap into the barrel till near racking time. This is a saving in cost, as taps are not cheap and one tap may be used for several barrels in turn, and it prevents any possible leakage as taps, like all wooden articles, will tend to dry out after a while. If the barrel is not provided with a tap right from the start of the fermentation, the tap opening in the lower part of the flat end will be closed with a cork which just fits, and can be hammered home making it fit flush with the outside of the barrel. When the wine is ready for tapping the tap is soaked for a few hours in water to swell up the wood and close up all cracks. The tap, which of course must fit the opening, is then held against the cork and hammered into the barrel.

Cork removal

When a corked barrel is tapped the cork will of course be pushed into the wine but this is not harmful. Corks can be removed when the barrel is empty at washing time, by suspending a loop of stout string in the empty barrel through the top bung hole and manœuvring the cork into the loop formed by the string by reversing the barrel. The string is then pulled quickly and the cork should come out.

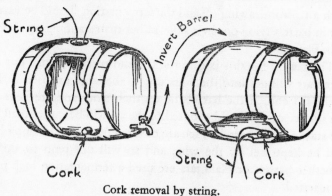

Cork removal by string.

The Wine Syphon

If for any reason it is not possible to draw off wine through a tap, as for instance if 1 gallon glass jars or 2 gallon stone jars or 10 gallon glass carboys are used, then it is desirable to fix up a syphon from a 4 ft. length of rubber tubing of diameter $\frac{3}{8}''$, preferably with a short length of glass tubing in each end. This piece of tubing is lowered into the wine until its end is about 1 inch above the base of the 1 gallon vessel or 3 to 4 inches over the bottom of the 10 gallon container so that it will not disturb the yeast deposit. The distances can be judged by measuring off the height externally and fixing a spring clip clothes peg to the rubber at the point where it emerges from the vessel.

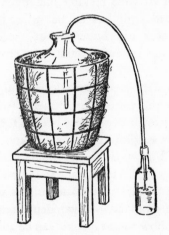

Drawing the wine off into bottles
by a syphon

The piece of tube outside the vessel is now held out sideways slanting slightly upwards so that the mouthpiece is just above the top of the vessel. Slight suction on the syphon by the mouth will fill the tube; then it should be firmly pinched near the outlet end and lowered quickly so that the outlet enters the opening of the vessel into which the wine is to pass. Provided the outlet is below the level of the liquid to be drawn off the wine will flow and continue flowing. To stop it flowing it is only necessary to lift the mouthpiece above the level of the liquid but it is preferable to draw the tube out from the vessel which is being racked as the liquid which runs back when the mouthpiece end is lifted may disturb the yeast deposit.

Commercially-made syphons are available which employ a squeeze bulb instead of suction with the mouth to cause the liquid to flow; modern ones are made entirely of plastic.

Fruit Pulpers

Some equipment is required for preparing the fruit and extracting the juice prior to wine making but much can be done by improvisation. Hard fruit has to be minced prior to pressing. A home mincer can be used but special apparatus for the purpose is made in Switzerland or Germany and can be imported.

The photograph of the small domestic fruit pulper obtained from Switzerland shows the various components (see plate 18). The centre roller with protruding spikes is used for hard fruit while the fluted roller is employed for grapes and other soft fruit. The fruit is pressed down on to the rollers which are turned by a handle. In a pulper of this type grape stalks will be automatically separated from the pulp. Home-made pulpers which work quite well can be made from an old wooden mangle and the two photographs show how such a mangle can be adapted for pulping grapes and other fruits (see plates 12 and 13).

First of all the mangle was removed from its stand and the rollers trimmed to within 2" of the ends by removing about ⅛" of wood along the surface of each roller. In addition the rollers can be fluted at 3" intervals or studded with stainless steel nails. That helps to catch the fruit and prevent grapes from riding up. It is desirable to build a wooden superstructure called a hopper to enable the fruit to fall on to the gap between the rollers.

Fruit Presses

Several types are available in this country and are illustrated herewith. The first is a small domestic press (see plate 15 and page 48)[1] but large enough to press about 40 lb. of apple pulp. The yield of juice should be round about 70 per cent.

The second press was imported from Switzerland, the various parts being clearly illustrated (see plate 16). The fruit is preferably placed in bags before pressing and the juice runs down the grooves on the inside of the basket. The loose bottom which lies on the base of the press is perforated and allows the juice to flow on to the grooves of the base and to run out. Such a press (see plate 17) cost about £4 0s. 0d. several years ago but duty is levied when bringing it into this country.

A somewhat larger press similar to those used in commerce but intended for domestic or farm use and suitable for pressing about 70 lb. of pulp is shown in plate 14. The pulp is folded into cloths made from wool which are supplied with the press. The cloths are folded over envelope fashion, and such an envelope of pulp is called a *cheese*. The envelope is held in position by frameworks of crossed slats which are placed between each cheese. A frame of slats is placed on top of the uppermost cheese and pressure is applied slowly and steadily. As the juice runs out more pressure can be applied. Such a press is very efficient and often purchased by wine makers who have formed a club or a circle and are thus able to purchase equipment co-operatively.

For bulk production power-operated presses such as that shown in the illustration will of course be required.

Some wine makers make their own presses or use a mangle to press the fruit. The pulp is put into a bag which exactly fits the mangle. The open end of the bag is folded over and fed in first.

The bag is then taken gently through the gap between the rollers. Care must be taken that an even layer of fruit passes between the rollers as if the fruit is pushed to the bottom of the bag this is

[1] Obtainable from Messrs. Joseph Bryant Ltd., P.O. Box 111, Bristol, 2.

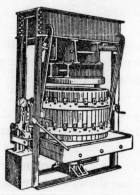

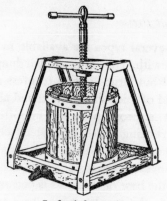

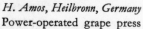

H. *Amos, Heilbronn, Germany*
Power-operated grape press

Loftus' domestic
fruit press

likely to burst. This method of pressing will not get the pulp quite dry in one go but some water can be added to the pulp and it can be passed through the rollers again.

A better method is to make a fruit press from wooden slats which are held together by a strong metal band. This slatted cylinder is stood on a flat wooden block suitably channelled, the pulp is transferred into it in bags of stout hessian, a stout board exactly fitting the cylinder is inserted and pressure applied to this board. A car jack can be used and the top of the jack can be held by a stout beam or protruding wall or by a strong frame fastened to the trough. Very considerable pressure has to be exerted and a car jack can provide this if it is given something sufficiently firm to press against. If pressure is applied too rapidly or too fiercely something will break rather than the juice be pressed out; also the bags will split and cause considerable annoyance. Pressure should only be applied gradually but as the juice runs out more pressure can be exerted.

An old copying press can also be used to press out the juice, the pulp being folded into cloths or bags and separated by a framework of crossed slats. The press is stood on a box in an open container, such as a barrel sawn in half, to catch the juice. Juice will start to exude at the first gentle pressure and pressure is applied gradually and at intervals. Better juice extraction is obtained by gentle pressure with gradual increases rather than by too great an initial pressure.

Care must be taken to ensure that all metal parts on presses or other apparatus which come into contact with the juice are either tinned or treated with an acid resisting lacquer.

Hydrometers

Once the juice has been prepared it has to be adjusted and the best way of doing so is to test the gravity of the juice and then add the required amount of syrup. As mentioned previously two hydrometers are required, one reading from 1·000 to 1·100 and another reading from 1·100 to 1·200. If it is desired to test the gravity of a strong syrup then a further hydrometer will be needed ranging from 1·200 to 1·300. It is possible to obtain a hydrometer which covers the complete range, i.e. which goes from 0·998 to 1·300, but naturally the accuracy of such an hydrometer is bound to be less than where hydrometers with a larger scale can be used. A hydrometer is illustrated in plate 20 and it is also shown how this instrument is floated in the juice or syrup to test its gravity. These hydrometers are made of glass and the broad end is weighted while the narrow tube which emerges carries a scale with figures on. The appropriate hydrometer is floated in the liquid in a measuring cylinder or hydrometer jar and it is important to stand this on a level table so that the hydrometer floats freely. Where the stem emerges at the surface of the liquid the reading is taken and that is in fact the gravity of the juice or syrup. The gravity as mentioned previously will vary with the sugar content of the juice and may be as low as 10 as for elderberries or as high as 70 for pears and round about 100 for grapes. The syrups on the other hand will have gravities ranging above 100 up to 300. Hydrometers are not difficult to use and in fact farmers who market milk are quite familiar with such an instrument. Even if the gravity of the juice has not been tested and a recipe is used which advocates dissolving sugar in the juice it is highly desirable to test the sugared juice before putting in the yeast. Recipes, as is obvious, can only be approximate due to the variation in the sugar content in the fruit, and one of the most frequent causes of failure in wine making is to start a fermentation with too high a gravity.

The Fermentation Lock

The most important piece of apparatus to the vintner and one which must be acquired is the fermentation lock. This little glass apparatus is not expensive and is easily obtainable. It is illustrated in plate 19. The trap is passed through a hole in a cork which can be of any size so as to fit either casks or gallon jars or even wine bottles. The lower rounded portion of the trap is filled with water containing some sulphite. A suitable strength sulphite solution is made by adding one Campden Tablet to a pint of water and some of this is poured into the lower portion of the lock. It is not desirable for the water to reach far into the bulbous part of the trap as otherwise some might be sucked back into the wine when gas ceases to be given off. This water seal or trap allows air or gas to bubble out but protects the wine from spoilage because no vinegar flies or undesirable bacteria can reach the wine.

Funnels, Measures etc.

The wine maker will require at least one funnel which should be either plastic or glass. He will also want some large china jugs and the old fashioned bedroom ewer can prove very useful. Otherwise little further equipment need be bought as basins and china jugs are generally available in most houses or can be borrowed as required. If enamel jugs are used care must be exercised to see that they are not chipped: any parts where the enamel has peeled off should be painted with a shellac varnish. If aluminium pans are used the juice should not remain too long in them as yeasts are sometimes inhibited by traces of aluminium. In fact most metals should be kept out of contact with fruit juices or wines at any stage in their manufacture; although copper

9. Bringing in the grapes for Port wine production

10. Treading grapes for Port wine production

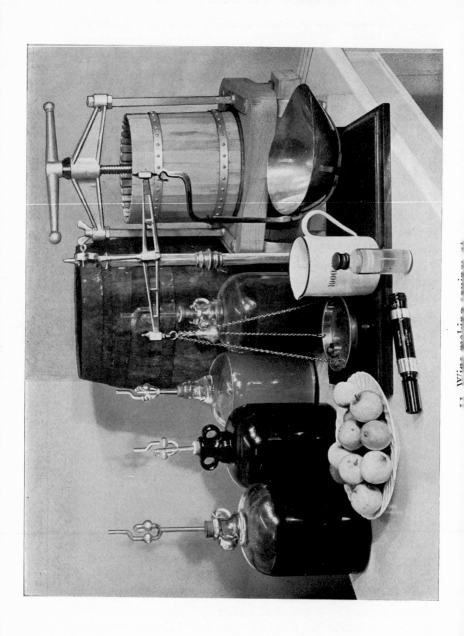

11. Wine-making equipment

vessels are often seen in wineries they are always tinned because tin is one of the few commoner metals that are harmless. Other accessories which may be required are rubber tubes, filter paper, asbestos for clarifying the wine and wooden sticks for stirring.

The care of Wine-Making Equipment

One of the most important tasks that the wine maker has to face is the care of his equipment. It is not only necessary to prevent mould growth in barrels but all wooden equipment will tend to retain traces of fruit juices and every care must be taken to sterilize the wood. Cleaning with hot soda water is the first step and then the wood should be well washed and thoroughly dried. Fruit presses and any other wooden equipment bar the casks are preferably coated with a good hard lacquer as that will keep them dry and thus prevent mould growth. Glass utensils such as hydrometers and measuring cylinders should always be washed immediately after use, and care must be taken that rubber tubes are washed well both inside and outside. It is far easier to prevent acetification in wine making than to correct any trouble once it has occurred.

Treatment of Barrels

Barrels are particularly prone to spoilage and care must be taken to clean them at once after emptying, again at intervals during the year, and prior to the vintage. In some districts barrels are stored empty after they have been thoroughly washed and treated with sulphur dioxide gas. This can be done by burning a sulphur wick in the barrel; after lighting the wick it is lowered into the barrel on a wire, the barrel bunged down for an hour or so. After removing the bung and wire the barrel is filled up with water and allowed to soak for about an hour, emptied, rinsed and stored in a dry shed. This treatment is open to the objection that such barrels may go mouldy after a while and need treatment at intervals or alternatively they may dry out and fall to pieces. All barrels which are left empty for a while will become leaky. Before use they have to be filled with water and soaked for some days, emptied, sulphited and washed. If it is possible to store barrels full then they must be stored filled with a preserving solution. Lime bisulphite, which is obtainable from brewers' sun-driesmen, is frequently used in the proportion of 1 pint to 20 gallons of water. Alternatively the vintner can make a sulphite solution from sodium metabisulphite using ½ lb. per 10 gallons and subsequently adding 1 oz. of citric acid to the barrel. This method is rather more expensive than burning a sulphur wick and after that filling up with water which is left standing in the barrel. When a smell of bad eggs is noted then the barrels have to be washed and treated again by one of the methods described, finally filling up with water and storing. If barrels have gone mouldy they must be steamed, washed out with hot soda solution and steamed again. The barrel is then soaked overnight with cold water and washed out next day. There must be no trace of a mouldy odour left in a barrel which is about to be used. Vinegar-sour barrels are treated similarly.

New barrels must be treated with steam and with hot soda water and well washed. Superior wines should not be stored in new barrels: these are preferably used for storing or fermenting cider or perry, or a lesser quality wine. After a year's use much of the undesirable bitter wood tannins will have been leached out of the wood.

THE PREPARATION OF THE MUST

All fruit juice intended for wine making is generically termed 'must'. There is grape must and apple must but most people will be more used to the word juice and one or the other term will be used indiscriminately. As mentioned earlier there are two methods of wine making, the white wine method where generally the juice only is fermented (though sometimes the fermentation is started in the presence of the pulp) and the red wine fermentation where nearly always the fermentation is carried out in the presence of the pulp for a shorter or longer period. Sometimes the pulp is heated to extract the colour and in that case it is pressed and only the juice is fermented.

Grape Must

Generally when grapes are fermented into wine no additions are made to the must prior to fermenting, with the exception of a little sulphite and a yeast starter. This of course makes wine making in grape growing countries fairly easy. In cold years or in cooler climates where even the juice of grapes may be unduly sour and lacking in sugar due to insufficient ripening, extra sugar has to be added.

Harvesting the Fruit

Wine making really starts in the vineyard. The quality and the type of wine that is obtained depends upon the method and the time of harvesting of the grapes. The finest white wines are made by selecting individual berries from the bunch and anyone who has watched the harvesting of grapes in Germany will have noticed that the harvesters carry a small tin hooked to their baskets. The bulk of the grapes go into the baskets but selected overripe ones are cut out from the bunch and dropped into the tin. Wines made from such berries are termed Ausleese (selectively gathered) wines. If the harvest is carried out rather later than the main harvest, wines made from grapes which may not have been harvested till all the leaves are fallen, are called Spätleese (gathered late) wines, while wines made from grapes which have raisinified are called Trockenbeere (dry berries) wines. In countries where grapes ripen well and where these really ripe grapes have turned mouldy, very fine wines are produced through the activity of this so-called 'noble mould'. The entire bunch is pressed as in this case one cannot remove the berries from the stems. When fermenting musts from mouldy berries a considerable quantity of sulphite has to be added to start with because this inhibits any further mould activity and allows the yeast to start fermenting. The grapes are sometimes pulped directly into fermenters in the vineyard instead of carting them back to the winery. This is done particularly in bad years when mould has attacked unripe grapes, so as not to give the mould time to spread further. In such cases a yeast starter and sulphite are added at once to the juice so as to ensure that the good wine yeast will predominate and thus ensure a sound fermentation. Whether the grapes are pressed in the vineyard or brought to the winery for pulping the juice should be pressed out without any delay. It is usual to put the pulp into a grape press without using cloths or sacks, but the amateur will be well advised to put his pulp into a bag before pressing. As the pulp, even after thorough pressing, will retain a considerable amount of juice some water may be added to the pulp prior to a second pressing.

In the case of red grapes for red wine, all the stems must be removed during pulping prior to fermentation. The entire pulp is put into a wide-necked container, such as a small barrel which has had one end removed. The pulp and juice are fermented in this vessel till the liquid is dark red. After about a week the pulp is pressed and the juice transferred to barrels or other similar containers. Care is taken to see that the container is full to the bung hole, the fermentation trap is inserted and the wine is allowed to ferment to dryness. It will clarify after a while or may have to be fined. After this the wine is racked at 3 or 4 monthly intervals.

Other Fruit Juices

When making wines from English fruit, the sugar content is invariably too low to give enough alcohol for the finished product to become a wine which will keep. Furthermore certain precautions have to be taken when using fruit which tends to get over-ripe and soft rather easily. Fruit as it ripens is frequently punctured by wasps or bees. As there are always yeasts on the surface of any fruit the juice which will be exposed through the skin of the fruit will inevitably start fermenting and just as surely as the alcohol is being formed fruit flies and vinegar bacteria will turn this alcohol to vinegar. The worst offender in this respect is the raspberry which often goes vinegar sour. It is not unusual to find a ripe raspberry which has become excessively sour and this sourness is mainly due to vinegar. Such fruit will be teeming with vinegar bacteria and even one sour berry can turn the rest of the wine to vinegar. There are two methods of preventing this; one is to bring the fruit to the boil and the other is to add at least one but preferably two Campden tablets to the gallon of juice. Campden tablets are not required for sterilization when the juice has been boiled as the heat will kill all bacteria present. But it has now been proved that the addition of one Campden tablet to the gallon will improve the quality of a wine.

Not all fruit juice for wine making can be prepared by simply pulping the fruit and pressing out the juice. Some fruit has to be softened by pouring boiling water over it or the juice can be drawn out by heat. Plums, cherries, gooseberries and rhubarb belong to this class. Fermentation is frequently carried out on the pulp for shorter or longer periods as this will cause the juice to become thin and facilitate pressing. Hard fruit like apples and pears require mincing after which the juice is pressed out. Dried fruit like raisins, figs and dates contain much sugar and because they are dried must be resoaked in water and are preferably brought to the boil and then well-pulped before pressing.

Vegetable Wines

Wine is frequently made from vegetables such as parsnips, beetroot, marrow and carrots. Vegetables are generally brought to the boil to soften the pulp before pressing. Sometimes components of a vegetable which are not used for cooking such as pea pods can be used for wine making. The leaves and tendrils of vines can also be turned into very good wine and some wine makers are very impressed with the quality of wine they obtain from parsley and lettuce. Vegetables contain insufficient amounts of sugar and acid for wine making so they have to be added while leaves contain no sugar at all. Potato wine is frequently very potent. This vegetable will ferment well but the potato content should be kept low as the wine will otherwise contain too much wood spirit and might prove harmful if drunk before maturing for a year or so.

Flower Wines

Very attractive wines can be made from elder-flowers and other flowers, such as cowslip and dandelion, all of which have a particular bouquet mainly due to the flowers used. But it is not possible to make a wine from sugar, flowers and water only because there would not be sufficient nourishment for the yeast, nor is there normally enough acid present so invariably some kind of fruit juice or dried fruit and some acid such as lemon juice or citric acid has to be added. Usually raisins are used and these being dried grapes not only add the necessary nutrient but provide added body and flavour to the special characteristic of the flower wine.

Bark and Tree Wines

The juice of the silver birch was used very extensively in ancient times for wine making and is still used in Baltic countries. The trees are tapped in March and the sap collected from the wound; as the juice is normally lacking in sugar and yeast nutrients these have to be added. Wines can also be made from sweet syrupy materials such as treacle, malt extract and honey provided the proper adjustments are made so that a suitable sugar content is attained. Provided the other adjuncts required to give a balanced wine, such as tannin and acid, are added, quite good wines can be prepared from such ingredients.

Cereal Wines

Rice, wheat and barley can all be used for wine making. Here again it is necessary to add some acid to the grain which has been swelled by boiling. Many wine makers add the juice of lemons and oranges while others use raisins or dates to add to the cereal mash.

Beer

It is possible to make wine from malt extract but this is preferably used for beer making either by itself or admixed with starchy material such as maize or rice. Beer is mainly produced from barley which has been sprouted and thus turned into malt. The principles underlying the making of beer are completely different from those of wine making and are therefore discussed in a separate section.

ADJUSTING THE MUST PRIOR TO WINE MAKING

As mentioned earlier wines may be either dry or sweet, sparkling or still, wines in which the alcohol content is entirely produced by fermentation or wines to which extra alcohol has been added. The vintner has the means of determining the type of wine he wishes to make whether he starts from grapes or any other ingredient. First of all he must adjust the juice to a suitable acidity and gravity. There is no reason why he should not follow the recipes which are given in the latter section of this book but it has been pointed out already that no recipe can be relied upon to produce the same result twice as it is affected by the amount of sugar which is normally present in the fruit and the state of ripeness at which the fruit is harvested. The riper the fruit the greater the sugar content and the less acid present.

TABLE I

THE SUGAR CONTENT OF VARIOUS FRUITS

Grapes both red and white contain from			15%–35%	of sugar
Red Currants contain from	.	.	3%–7%	,,
White Currants ,,	,,	.	4½%–5½%	,,
Black Currants ,,	,,	.	7½%–8½%	,,
Gooseberries ,,	,,	.	3½%–7½%	,,
Strawberries ,,	,,	.	5%–7%	,,
Apples ,,	,,	.	9%–15%	,,
Plums ,,	,,	.	4%–12%	,,
Blackberries ,,	,,	.	5½%–6%	,,
Raspberries ,,	,,	.	4½%–7½%	,,
Cherries ,,	,,	.	7½%–12½%	,,
Figs ,,	approx.	.	50%	,,
Raisins ,,	,,	.	60%	,,
Dates ,,	,,	.	70%	,,

TABLE II

THE ACID CONTENT OF VARIOUS FRUITS

Grapes both red and white contain from			0·3%–2·5%	Acid
Red Currants contain from	.	.	1½%–3%	,,
White Currants ,,	,,	.	1½%–3%	,,
Black Currants ,,	,,	.	1½%–3%	,,
Gooseberries ,,	,,	.	1%–1½%	,,
Strawberries ,,	,,	.	¾%–1%	,,
Apples ,,	,,	.	½%–1½%	,,
Plums ,,	,,	.	½%–1¾%	,,
Blackberries ,,	,,	.	¾%–2%	,,
Raspberries ,,	,,	.	1¼%–2½%	,,
Cherries ,,	,,	.	1½%–1¾%	,,
Figs	.	.	Low	
Raisins	.	.	,,	
Dates	.	.	,,	

Adjusting the sugar and acid content of various fruit juices

A comparison of the sugar contents of various fruits is interesting and shows the variations which may be expected. As the sugar content increases the gravity of the juice will increase and hence less sugar has to be added.

The sugar content is not the only factor which has to be taken into consideration. Some fruits are so sour that considerable amounts of water or sugar water have to be added to make a wine which will be pleasant to drink. In that case the sugar present in the fruit may have been reduced so much by dilution that no heed need be taken of the amount originally present. Reference to Tables I and II will soon clarify this point. When referring to the above tables it will be noticed for instance that white and red currants can have as much as 3 per cent of acid. This is much too high and generally $\frac{1}{2} - \frac{3}{4}$ per cent should be aimed at. Short of analysing the juice the wine maker has to rely on taste to decide how much to dilute the juice so as to obtain a wine which will be pleasant to drink. It must be remembered that a sweet juice will taste less sour even with the same amount of acid present than a juice containing no sugar. Hence it is as well to sweeten a juice prior to tasting by adding a tablespoonful of sugar to four tablespoonfuls of juice and warming slightly to dissolve the sugar. If it is unbearably sour, then an equal amount of water should be added to reduce the sourness but another tablespoonful of sugar will be needed to bring the sweetening up again. If after this adjustment the juice tastes just right then for wine making the juice will have to be diluted by an equal amount of water or syrup. On the other hand should the juice be still too sour then four tablespoonfuls of the juice just tasted are again mixed with an equal amount of water and one more tablespoonful of sugar added before the juice is tasted. This second dilution will have reduced the acidity to a quarter the original amount; this is best seen by referring to the acid content of the juice expressed in percentages. Say, for instance, a juice contains 2 per cent of acid; the first dilution will reduce that to 1 per cent and the second to $\frac{1}{2}$ per cent.

This is about the amount of acid which should be present for a dry wine; a sweet wine may contain a little more without tasting too sour. If on the other hand a juice contains only $1\frac{1}{2}$ per cent of acid then the first dilution will bring the acid down to $\frac{3}{4}$ per cent which would still be rather sour but after the second dilution, which corresponds to an acidity of $\frac{3}{8}$ per cent, the wine will prove rather insipid. In such a case only two parts of syrup or water should be added to one part of juice, i.e. the juice is diluted a third instead of adding three parts of syrup or water to one of juice, resulting in a dilution of the juice amounting to one quarter. Dilution with syrup instead of water is usually preferable.

To avoid undue dilution for the reduction of acidity some of the acid can be removed by chemical means prior to fermentation. This is best done by the addition of some chalk and $\frac{1}{4}$ to $\frac{1}{2}$ oz. to a gallon of juice will reduce the acidity by about $\frac{1}{4}$ to $\frac{1}{2}$ per cent. The chalk should be pure medicinal chalk obtained from a chemist or preferably powdered cuttle fish which is less likely to clog up a filter. This is first rubbed down to a smooth paste with a little juice and then stirred into the bulk of the juice. The liquid will start to foam because gas is given up by the chalk as it neutralizes some of the acid; obviously this must be done in a vessel from which some of the juice has been removed to allow adequate headspace for the foam. The insoluble salts formed from the interaction of the chalk and acid will gradually settle but as this may take some time the fermentation is usually proceeded with and the precipitate is removed along with the bulk of the yeast at the first racking.

The vintner is advised not to exceed the $\frac{1}{2}$ oz. of chalk per gallon referred to above and it is always preferable to apply this method of de-acidification to the juice before fermentation rather than to the finished wine because in the latter case it can sometimes affect the flavour slightly. In the case of wines made from grapes the addition of chalk helps in the removal of tartaric acid, some of which is normally precipitated during maturing, but the addition of chalk before fermentation is more effective than subsequent addition.

Should a finished wine be found to be too acid so that treatment with chalk is necessary, it must be remembered that up to six weeks may be needed for the calcium precipitate to settle, so the wine must be stored for this period and then be racked again; this period may however be shortened by refrigeration.

Young wines from grapes can also be made less acid by stirring up the yeast deposit and bringing the wine into a warm place. This starts what is known as a 'malo-lactic' fermentation. The malic

TABLE III

SUGAR ADDITIONS FOR THE PRODUCTION OF GRAPE WINES OF DIFFERENT STRENGTHS
(From *Le Vin*, by E. Chancrin)

Note: This table applies only to grape juice. Sugared fruit juices will yield wines of a higher alcohol content.

Sp. Gr. of Grape Juice	Gravity	Approx. percentage of Sugar (wt-vol)	Approx. percentage of Alcohol (by vol) which will be produced from the sugar	Approx. amount of sugar to be added to one gallon to increase Alcohol to (by vol)			Approx. amount of sugar to be added to ten gallons to increase Alcohol to (by vol)		
				10% oz.	14% oz.	18% oz.	10% lb. oz.	14% lb. oz.	18% lb. oz.
1·050	50	10·3	6·0	11	20	32	7 0	12 8	20 0
1·055	55	11·6	6·8	9	17	29	5 10	10 10	18 2
1·060	60	13·0	7·6	7	15	27	4 6	9 6	16 14
1·065	65	14·3	8·4	5	13	25	3 2	8 2	15 10
1·070	70	15·6	9·2	3	11	23	1 14	6 14	14 6
1·075	75	17·0	10·0	—	10	21	—	6 4	13 2
1·080	80	18·3	10·8	—	8	20	—	5 0	12 8
1·085	85	19·6	11·5	—	6	18	—	3 12	11 4
1·090	90	21·0	12·3	—	4	16	—	2 8	10 0
1·095	95	22·3	13·1	—	2	14	—	1 4	8 12
1·100	100	23·6	13·9	—	—	12	—	—	7 8
1·105	105	25·0	14·7	—	—	10	—	—	6 4
1·110	110	26·3	15·5	—	—	8	—	—	5 0
1·115	115	27·6	16·2	—	—	6	—	—	3 12
1·120	120	29·0	17·0	—	—	4	—	—	2 8
1·125	125	30·3	17·8	—	—	2	—	—	1 4
1·130	130	31·6	18·5	—	—	—	—	—	—

acid is converted by bacterial action into the less sour lactic acid.

Rhubarb contains an acid which, if taken in quantity, can be harmful but it is quite easy to remove this by means of chalk. This will be fully discussed in the recipe for rhubarb wine.

Cases can also occur, particularly in vegetable and flower wines which will be considered later, where the wine contains insufficient acid. Then it is necessary to add a little acid, citric acid being preferred. To increase the acidity by approximately ¼ per cent add ⅛ oz. of citric acid to each gallon of juice.

Adjusting the sugar content of grape juice to produce wines of different alcohol content

The amount of sugar which has to be added to a grape juice will vary with the amount which is naturally present in the juice. If the juice is not too sour then the sugar is added in the solid state and care taken to ensure that all the sugar is dissolved. When sugar is dissolved in any liquid, be it water or fruit juice, it will not only increase the gravity of the juice but it will also add to the volume, or in other words bulk, of the liquid. This increase has to be allowed for by referring to Table IV or by calculating the increase which will result. This is quite easy as it is known that sugar occupies six-tenths of its weight in volume. Therefore, the weight in ounces is multiplied by 0·6 to obtain the volume in fluid ounces.

40 oz. × 0·6—24 oz. or in other words

40 oz. of sugar will occupy 24 fl. oz. in volume.

TABLE IV

COMPARISON BETWEEN THE WEIGHT AND THE VOLUME
OF SUGAR AFTER SOLUTION

10 oz. of sugar occupy a volume of 6 fl. oz. on solution
16 oz. (1 lb.) of sugar occupy a volume of 10 fl. oz. (¼ pint) on solution
32 oz. (2 lb.)   „   „   „   20 „   (1 pint)   „
64 oz. (4 lb.)   „   „   „   40 „   (2 pints)   „

The gravity increases also with sugar addition and from Table III it is easily seen that the more sugar is added the stronger will a wine become. On the first line of this table it is noted that the gravity of 50 or the specific gravity of 1.050 is equivalent to a sugar concentration in the juice of approximately 10·3 per cent. When all this has fermented and the wine is entirely free from sugar then the alcohol content would be about 6 per cent by volume or just under 5 per cent by weight. If on the other hand 11 oz. of sugar are added to a gallon of juice then the alcohol content will increase to 10 per cent. If 20 oz. are added the resulting wine will contain 14 per cent of alcohol and if 33 oz. are added the alcohol content will be more and may be as much as 18 per cent. Yeast will not ferment to this high alcohol content if the entire amount of sugar is added at the start of fermentation but the wine is likely to have an alcohol content at first of round about 14 to 15 per cent and a residual sweetness of round about 8 per cent. Such a wine, if it has been fermented very slowly with a Sauterne Yeast, will be somewhat Sauterne-like in flavour, particularly after maturing for some considerable time. If one wishes to obtain a wine with 18 per cent of alcohol then extra yeast nutrient is required and the sugar should be added in several lots say 4 oz. at a time. These 4 oz. are added when the fermentation has been vigorous for 3–10 days and juice on tasting has lost nearly all its sweetness. It must be remembered though that when adding sugar directly to a fermenting liquid it must be well stirred in. If this is not done it is quite easy to spoil the yeast, especially when it is a sedimentary yeast, as the sugar is heavy and will sink to the bottom of the fermentation vessel forming a layer of strong syrup which will kill or weaken the yeast, and so the fermentation will become sluggish or even cease.

Adjustment of other fruit juices prior to fermentation

Grape juice is comparatively easy to convert into wine provided the grapes have ripened sufficiently so that the juice ultimately reaches a gravity of no less than 85 degrees. Anything below that

will result in a wine with too little alcohol and hence of poor keeping power. High gravities are not normal for other fruits with the
exception of figs, raisins and dates, and hence considerable sugar
addition will have to be made for most fruits. For a dry light wine
a sugar content of 20 per cent is desirable, while for a sweet wine
as much as 40 per cent will be needed. As explained earlier the
alcohol content of a wine will be approximately half the original
sugar content and therefore 20 per cent will equal a wine with
approximately 10 per cent of alcohol (more accurately $20 \times$
$0.46 = 9.2$ per cent alcohol by weight or $20 \times .57 = 11.4$ per cent
alcohol by volume). When the sugar content is 40 per cent not all
of this will be converted into alcohol as under normal conditions
of fermentation 20 per cent of alcohol (more accurately 18.4 per
cent by weight or 22.8 per cent by volume) is more than will be
produced by yeast. In the first instance one can only reckon on
$14\frac{1}{2}$ per cent to $15\frac{1}{2}$ per cent of alcohol by volume. That is, only
threequarters of the sugar in the juice will be turned to alcohol
and 10 per cent will remain behind unfermented to form a sweet
wine.

If reference is made to Tables I and II it will be seen that there
are many juices which are not so sour as to require the addition of
extra water. In the case of strawberry juice the sugar content is
normally about 5 per cent (from 4.5 per cent to 7 per cent). The
sugar content of this juice will need to be increased to 20 per cent
if a dry wine of suitable alcohol content is desired. To calculate
the amount of sugar to be added needs a little thought. When a
juice contains 5 per cent of sugar this means 5 oz. of sugar in
100 fl. oz. (5 pints) of juice—that is 5 per cent weight/volume.
1 lb. of sugar made up to 1 gallon (160 fl. oz.) makes a 10 per cent
solution of sugar weight/volume. So we would assume that if
$1\frac{1}{2}$ lb. of sugar is dissolved in sufficient strawberry juice to make
exactly one gallon we should have 20 per cent of sugar (15 per
cent plus 5 per cent) in the liquid. Actually this is not quite correct
because the sugar occupies 24 oz. $\times 0.6 = 14.6$ fl. oz. so that this
much less strawberry juice is required; using less juice will de-
crease the amount of sugar according to the sugar content of the

juice. This error, however, is too small to be of importance in wine making. The error that must be avoided is that of adding 1½ lb. of sugar *to* a gallon of the juice because we shall then have more than a gallon, actually 160 oz. plus 14·4 oz. which will give a total sugar content of 18·8 per cent instead of 20 per cent.

As great accuracy is not usually needed, the simpler method of arriving at the amount of sugar to be added can be used and a little extra (say 4 oz. in the above example) can be added to make up for the error.

Actually strawberries make a far better dessert wine than table wine and consequently more sugar than the above is needed and for one gallon of juice about 4 to 4½ lb. of sugar are required to give a wine with 17 per cent to 18 per cent of alcohol and sufficient residual sweetness. As strawberries are expensive, a cheaper and frankly just as good wine can be made by adding some water in which the sugar can be dissolved. For the sake of convenience in Tables V and VI adjustments for wines are given in such quantities that the adjusted juice will measure a gallon. Suppose to produce a strawberry dessert wine 4 pints of strawberry juice are mixed with 4 pints of a syrup which contains 40 oz. of sugar. Since 4 pints is equal to 80 oz., the syrup contains 50 per cent of sugar (weight/volume). When this syrup is diluted with an equal quantity of strawberry juice, the sugar contents of the strawberry juice and of the syrup are halved. Say the strawberry juice contains 7·0 per cent of sugar this when halved will amount to 3½ per cent and when added to 25 per cent, the sugar content of the adjusted juice will be 28½ per cent. To obtain the amount of alcohol by volume the sugar content is multiplied by 0·57. The wine will therefore contain 17 per cent of alcohol. *High alcohol content is best obtained by fermenting in the presence of the fruit, by adding additional yeast nutrient, and by adding the syrup in several lots.* If 4 pints of syrup are given in the recipe, then only 2 pints are used at the start of the fermentation. The remaining two pints are added when the fermentation has passed its peak. By using a sugar solution rather than solid sugar, wine making is much facilitated. First of all it is easy to calculate the amount required from the gravity of the juice and of the syrup; secondly, as there will be no increase of volume due to added solid sugar, the wine maker can work out the amounts needed to give the desired volume for fermenting, and thirdly, the syrup can be added in two stages, thus allowing the primary fermentation to proceed with some headroom and enabling the wine maker to fill the container to the top with the residual syrup. Sometimes, even after the addition of the second lot of syrup, the fermentation is very vigorous and spills out through the fermentation trap. If this happens some of the brew is removed to another container for a while and returned to the bulk when the fermentation has quietened down.

The proportions of syrup to be used for the production of a strawberry dessert wine with 17 per cent alcohol which were given above were only sufficient for a dry wine. If a sweet wine is desired then a stronger syrup can be used or the finished wine can be sweetened by some solid sugar, but in this latter case there is always the possibility of a renewal of fermentation. If a 60 per cent sugar syrup instead of a 50 per cent had been used then this 10 per cent excess sugar would be halved as only 4 pints of syrup are used in one gallon. Hence the wine will have a residual sweetness amounting to 5 per cent of sugar which is about right for a semi-sweet dessert wine.

Just as in jam making different recipes can be used, so will recipes for wine making vary. Some wine makers will prefer to use solid sugar rather than syrup but if a strong syrup with a gravity of 300 is used the amount of water that is added is really quite small. In the above example where a sweet wine with a high alcohol content requiring much sugar is produced with syrup, the amount of water that is introduced with the syrup amounts to two pints. As will be seen later a syrup of gravity 300 is produced by dissolving 4 lb. of sugar in 2 pints of water. As it is known that 4 lb. of sugar occupy 2 pints, it is quite clear that this amount of sugar will produce 4 pints of syrup. If the wine maker wishes he could alter his recipe, instead of using 4 pints of strawberry juice and 4 pints of syrup to produce a gallon of wine he could use 6

12. Fruit pulper made from an old mangle

13. Showing the rollers converted for pulping

14. Beare's small hand-operated fruit press

15. Beare's Miniature fruit press

16. Components of a Swiss press showing construction

17. A Swiss press ready for use

pints of strawberry juice and 4 lb. of sugar. The total volume will then be again 8 pints or 1 gallon.

It is always desirable to use the strongest syrup possible, unless the juice is excessively sour and requires dilution with water when it will be easier to use a weaker syrup to give the required dilution and at the same time the required sugar content. Care must be taken not to add an excessive amount of water or syrup. Whenever possible very sour juices, such as that of red currants, should be blended with one less sour like that of strawberries as this will produce a wine with more body than one made with too much water. Furthermore, the addition of much water frequently results in a sluggish or incomplete fermentation as the available yeast nutrients will be reduced by dilution and be insufficient for adequate yeast growth. Although added yeast nutrients assist the fermentation they are by themselves inadequate for proper yeast growth and it is essential to have enough natural yeast foods present such as are contained in a fruit juice which has not been unduly diluted to ensure a sound fermentation. Also, in many cases, it is preferable to ferment for a few days in the presence of the pulp as the wine will then have more body and taste fuller and it will also prove more economical as the yield of juice will be greater. The exceptions to this are wines made from pears, apples and white currants where the juice only is fermented, while in the case of rhubarb or of vegetables such as parsnip, carrots and beet it is better to press these after softening by boiling water or by boiling and to ferment the resulting juice.

The amount of time that should be given to pulp fermentation depends on the taste and astringency of the fruit. If a fruit is very bitter and stringent, such as is the case with sloes, then approximately one day will be sufficient but with a mild fruit like strawberries 4 to 5 days is not too long. The decision when to press can only be arrived at by tasting the fermenting juice. Pressing has also to be frequently delayed till sufficient colour has been extracted. Furthermore, during the fermentation the pulp will have become less tough and pressing will therefore be facilitated and will result in a better yield of juice.

TABLE V

SUGAR OR SYRUP ADDITIONS FOR THE PRODUCTION OF DRY FRUIT WINES HAVING AN ORIGINAL GRAVITY OF 90 TO 100

Fruit used	Gravity of juice	Amount of juice or pulp Pints	Amount of syrup Pints	Gravity of syrup	Type of Yeast	Yeast nutrient
Apple	50	6½	1½	300	Wine or Champagne	½ teaspoonful
Apple	60	6¾	1¼	300	,,	½ ,,
Pear	60	6¾	1¼	300	Wine or Pommard	½ ,,
Raspberry	40	4	4	160		½ ,,
Blackberry	35	5	3	210	,,	½ ,,
Loganberry	35	4	4	170	,,	½ ,,
Red Currants (2 parts red 1 part black)	50	3	5	160	,,	1
White currant (not on pulp) juice only	40	3	5	130	,,	1
Bilberry	35	4	4	180	Wine	1
Rhubarb	15	5½	2½	300	Wine or Sauterne	½
Strawberry	55	6	2	280	Wine	½

This table covers the gravities of juices ranging from 15 to 60 degrees and is intended to be used as a general guide. Where the gravity of the juice is not in accordance with the table suitable allowance must be made.

TABLE VI

SUGAR OR SYRUP ADDITIONS FOR THE PRODUCTION OF SWEET FRUIT WINES HAVING AN ORIGINAL GRAVITY OF 150 TO 160

Fruit used	Gravity of juice	Amount of juice	Amount of syrup	Gravity	Type of Yeast	Yeast nutrient
		Pints	Pints			
Blackcurrant	50	4½	3½	300	Wine or Pommard	1 teaspoonful
Blackberry	35	4¼	3¾	300	Sherry, Port or Madeira	1 ,,
Bilberry	35	4¼	3¾	300	Port	2 ,,
Gooseberry	35	4¼	3¾	300	Sherry	1 ,,
Strawberry	55	4½	3½	300	Sherry	1 ,,
Cherry	60	5	3	300	Wine or Port	1 ,,
Damson	55	4½	3½	300	Port or Malaga	1 ,,
Rhubarb	15	3½	4½	300	Sauterne or Tokay	1 ,,
Apple	50	4½	3½	300	Sauterne or Tokay	1 ,,
Plum	60	5	3	300	Sherry	1 ,,
Elderberry	35	4¼	3¾	300	Port or Malaga	1 ,,

N.B. If the must is rich in fruit content then a gravity of 150 will ferment out. Should the gravity be higher it is preferable to add the syrup in two lots.

Determination of Sugar additions

Generally it is quite sufficient to refer to Tables IV, V and VI or to subsequent recipes to decide how much syrup or sugar has to be added to a juice. On the other hand there are many vintners who wish to design their own wine recipes, using a mixture of ingredients like parsnips or other vegetables or perhaps even wheat, together with raisins and the juice of various fruits such as lemons and oranges and spices such as ginger or cloves. When a mixture of ingredients is used then they must be well soaked in boiling water and left for a day or two. All ingredients should be well pulped before pressing. Such a mixture will have to be adjusted for acidity as unless plenty of lemons have been used the acid content will be low. The juice must be tested for its gravity and sugar or syrup be added in accordance with tables V or VI. In these tables various gravities to produce either a dry or a sweet wine are shown and there is sure to be one corresponding with the chosen mixture. Then a device known as the 'Pearson Square', the use of which is illustrated in the following example, may be employed to assist in the calculation.

Use of the Pearson Square for adjusting the gravity of juice with syrup of known gravity

In this example it is assumed that the juice has an initial gravity of 50 and that the syrup available has a gravity of 300

Gravity of Syrup	Parts of Syrup
(A) 300	50 (D)
(C) 100	
(B) 50	200 (E)
Gravity of Juice	Parts of Juice

To employ the Pearson Square five successive steps must be followed.

1. Place in the upper left hand corner of a square at (A) the gravity of the syrup to be used = 300.

2. In the lower left hand corner at (B) place the gravity of juice = 50.

3. In the centre of the square at (C) place the desired gravity = 100.

4. Now subtract the centre figure from the figure in the upper left hand corner and place the remainder at (E) in the lower right hand corner (300 − 100 = 200).

5. Subtract the figure in the lower left hand corner from the figure in the centre of the square and place the remainder at (D) in the upper right hand corner (100 − 50 = 50).

This last figure (50) is the number of parts of the syrup of gravity 300 required to be added to 200 parts of juice of gravity 50 to give a juice of gravity 100.

Expressed in other words, 1 pint of strong syrup has to be added to 4 pints of juice. If one is working in one gallon jars 1½ pints of syrup and 6 pints of juice would not be sufficient to ensure filling the container so use 6½ pints of juice and 1¾ pints of syrup.

The Pearson Square is quite easy to understand but the following formula is an alternative and may be preferred by some.

To bring say 10 gallons of a juice with a gravity of 50 to a gravity of 100 using a syrup of gravity 300 the calculation is as follows:

The formula to employ is $D = E \times \dfrac{C - B}{A - C}$

where D = quantity of syrup which has to be added.

E = quantity of juice to be sugared.

B = gravity of juice.

C = desired gravity of sugared juice.

A = gravity of syrup to be used.

Table VII—SYRUP TABLES

This table shows the quantity of sugar and water to make a gallon of syrup of known gravity.

Specific Gravity	*Gravity*	*Degrees Brix or per cent Sugar by weight*	*To produce 1 gallon syrup*			
			Sugar		*Water*	
			lb.	*oz.*	*pt.*	*oz.*
1·070	70	16·2	1	14	7	2
1·080	80	18·2	2	2¼	6	18½
1·090	90	20·2	2	6½	6	16
1·100	100	23·9	2	10½	6	13
1·110	110	26·0	2	15	6	10
1·115	115	27·1	3	1½	6	9
1·120	120	28·1	3	3½	6	7½
1·125	125	29·1	3	5½	6	6½
1·130	130	30·2	3	7¾	6	5
1·135	135	31·2	3	10	6	3½
1·140	140	32·3	3	12	6	2½
1·145	145	33·3	3	14	6	1
1·150	150	34·3	4	0	6	0
1·155	155	35·3	4	2½	5	18½
1·160	160	36·3	4	4½	5	17
1·165	165	37·3	4	6¾	5	15½
1·170	170	38·3	4	9	5	14¼
1·175	175	39·3	4	11	5	13
1·180	180	40·3	4	13	5	11½
1·185	185	41·3	4	15½	5	10¼
1·190	190	42·2	5	1½	5	9
1·195	195	43·1	5	3½	5	7½
1·200	200	44·1	5	5¾	5	6
1·205	205	45·0	5	8	5	4¾
1·210	210	46·0	5	10	5	3½
1·215	215	46·9	5	12	5	2
1·220	220	47·8	5	14	5	0¾
1·225	225	48·7	6	0½	4	19½
1·230	230	49·6	6	2½	4	18
1.235	235	50·5	6	4¾	4	16¾
1·240	240	51·4	6	7	4	15½
1·245	245	52·3	6	9	4	14
1·250	250	53·2	6	11	4	12¾
1·260	260	55·0	6	15½	4	10
1·270	270	56·7	7	3¾	4	7½
1·280	280	58·5	7	8	4	4¾
1·290	290	60·2	7	12¼	4	2
1·300	300	61·8	8	0½	3	19½
1·310	310	63·5	8	5	3	17
1·330	330	66·8	8	13½	3	11¼

Thus in the above example

$$D = 10 \text{ gallons} \times \frac{100 - 50}{300 - 100}$$

$$= 10 \times \frac{50}{200} \text{ or } 10 \times \frac{1}{4} = 2\tfrac{1}{2} \text{ gallons of syrup}$$

to be added to 10 gallons of juice.

Adjusting high gravity syrups and juices to lower gravities

Sometimes a fruit juice, on account of its high acid content, has to be diluted with an equal volume of syrup. If a syrup of a gravity of 300 is available but a lower gravity is required then it is quite easy to calculate the amount of water which has to be added. Say for instance, the juice has a gravity of 50. As only half will be used the effective gravity will be half, i.e. 25. If it is intended to produce a juice with a gravity of 100 then 100 − 25 leaves a gravity of 75. The syrup, of which again only half the volume will have to be used, will therefore have to have a gravity of 150, that is 2 × 75 so as to amount to a gravity of 75 when halved. To reduce 300 to 150 is, of course, quite simple as the addition of an equal quantity of water will halve the gravity. When a less convenient figure is required, say a syrup of gravity 125, then the law of proportion will assist. If 150 parts are diluted to 300 the gravity will be 150. Similarly 125 diluted to 300 the gravity will be 125. These proportions can be reduced to any convenient measure, say $\frac{150}{10}$ and $\frac{300}{10}$ equal 15 parts and 30 parts or $7\tfrac{1}{2}$ parts and 15 parts. These parts can be pints or any other convenient quantity.

Sometimes a grape juice or an extract of raisins or other dried fruit has too high a gravity. In that case the extract or juice must be diluted with water, as follows:

Say a gravity of 100 is required and the juice has a gravity of 125. By taking a 100 or 10 or 1 parts and increasing it by the addition of water to 125 or $12\tfrac{1}{2}$ or $1\tfrac{1}{4}$ parts the gravity of a 125 will be reduced to 100.

Addition of Acid and Yeast nutrient

All pure fruit juices prior to dilution contain sufficient natural yeast food to enable yeast to grow. When dilution is brought about by adding syrup or sugar some extra yeast nutrient may have to be added. Added yeast nutrients such as ammonium phosphate are only of value if natural organic yeast foods are also present. If these are lacking such organic nutrients can be supplied by the addition of pure malt extract. About 2 or 4 teaspoonfuls per gallon will normally suffice. If the fruit juice is diluted by water or syrup then $\frac{1}{2}$ to 1 teaspoonful of ammonium phosphate or other similar yeast nutrient will stimulate yeast growth. When it is desired to produce a yeast starter then pure fruit juice to which only a small amount of sugar has been added is the best method of propagating the yeast, but failing fruit juice 1 ounce of malt extract and 1 ounce of sugar in $\frac{3}{4}$ pint of water will serve equally well as a medium for growth. Most fruit juices contain sufficient acid but where acid is lacking then some must be added. The best acid for this purpose is citric acid and the amount which has to be added to a non-acid liquid such as is produced from roots and flowers ranges from $\frac{1}{2}$ per cent for a dry wine to $\frac{3}{4}$ per cent for a sweet wine. $\frac{1}{2}$ per cent is equivalent to $\frac{1}{2}$ oz. in 5 pints or about $\frac{3}{4}$ oz. in a gallon. $\frac{3}{4}$ per cent is about $1\frac{1}{4}$ oz. in a gallon. Many fruit juices may need a little additional acid when they have been adjusted by syrup but it is best to test them for acid content by the method described on page 181.

Yeast starters in wine making

Although most fruit juices will contain some yeast cells, which can only be entirely removed or killed by boiling, these yeasts are not usually able to produce a wine with a high alcohol content. Furthermore these natural yeasts are always accompanied by a variety of undesirable moulds and bacteria which lead to off flavours and spoilage of the wine. The addition of sulphite suppresses many of the weaker yeasts and bacteria and may allow the more active wine yeasts to dominate the fermentation, but eventually, undesirable complications may arise. One method of overcoming this trouble which is practised in many wine-making countries where there are far more wine yeasts in the atmosphere than in this country, is to prepare a 'Pieds de Cuve'. This, translated into English, is 'The feet of the fermentation'. A few days prior to the vintage some very clean ripe grapes are picked, the juice is pressed and sulphited. This, as already indicated, will inhibit the weaker yeasts and the strong wine yeasts will eventually start to work. This brew is then used to start the bulk of the fermentation; in fact, the fermentation of that vintage rests firmly on 'the feet of the original brew' which by being already in an active state of fermentation from the stronger wine yeasts will dominate the fermentation. Another method, and a far more reliable one, especially in this country where wine yeasts are not prevalent in the fruit, is to use a pure yeast culture of known type. A number of pure wine yeasts originally obtained from continental yeast laboratories are being cultured in this country now and supplied for a nominal charge to wine makers by the Grey Owl Research Laboratories. Once a culture has been propagated in the suggested small quantity of juice then more juice can be added to increase the original amount to 10, 20 or as much as 50 times the quantity and so on. The yeast deposit can be used again for further fermentation but only during the same season. It is advisable to acquire a fresh culture each year.

LIST OF SELECTED WINE YEASTS

As with all other living organisms various varieties of yeasts exist and they are, to a certain extent, characteristic of particular areas where they are largely responsible for the wine types specific to those areas. They can, of course, be cultivated and kept as a pure strain which can be transported anywhere. The following list of selected yeasts represent a few of the many available and have been chosen as those which give the best flavours and also as the most easy for the amateur to use.

By far the most convenient for general use is the All Purpose Wine Yeast. This is a sedimentary type, that is it settles readily on standing so that the wine can be easily decanted or syphoned off without much waste and with almost complete separation from the yeast. It is easily the best for white table wines and entirely suitable for red table wines but for the very deep red wines the Pommard yeast will retain the colour even better and give a characteristic flavour.

The All Purpose Yeast will also make a satisfactory Champagne but it will not be possible to remove the yeast formed in the bottle by the usual champagne method; to do this a Champagne yeast is essential.

For the sweet, strongly flavoured white dessert wines Sauterne or Tokay yeasts are advocated.

Sherries, whether dry or sweet, can be made with various yeasts provided the sherry technique is followed, but the best flavours are always obtained by the use of a proper Sherry yeast.

The fortified types of sweet wines such as Port, Malaga, Madeira, whether or not the amateur intends to fortify, are most successful if made with the appropriate yeast.

For cider a fast-working yeast is desirable and Herrliberg is recommended. Alternatively a Champagne yeast is suitable and either yeast can be used for perry.

Wine yeasts are not suitable for beer making and of the many beer yeasts which exist the sedimentary Lager Beer yeast is strongly recommended.

Recommended Wine Yeasts

All Purpose, Chablis, Hock	For Table Wines, White and Rosé
Pommard, Burgundy	For Red Wines
Sauterne, Tokay	For Sweet White Dessert Wines
Port	For Port
Malaga, Madeira	For Fortified Sweet Wines
Sherry, Sherry Flor	For Sweet and Dry Sherries

Champagne	For Champagne
Herrliberg	For Sparkling Wines, Cider, Perry
Maury, Mead	For Mead, but All Purpose Yeast preferred
Lager Beer, Stout, Ale	For Beer

These yeast cultures can be kept in a cool place (or a refrigerator) for some months but must be activated before use.

Pure wine yeast cultures as fermentation starters

Formerly wine yeasts were only available in the form of agar slants on which the yeasts were grown. These slants are supplied in test tubes and are known as tube cultures or in bottles known as bottle cultures. Tube cultures are still available and the yeast grown in this way is particularly active. If the agar slant is loosened and transferred to a gallon jar of prepared must which is free from other yeasts then the fermentation will start within 24 hours which shows how active a yeast is when grown on agar. However it is not suggested that this method be used unless the must has been freed from other yeast by boiling. Wild yeasts are invariably present in the must prepared from fruits or vegetables and the only way to ensure that the wine yeast will dominate the fermentation is to add it in an actively fermenting state prepared as a starter in a small volume of sterilised fruit juice. This is normally prepared in a bottle of 10 or 12 oz. capacity. About 4 oz. of orange juice is mixed with an equal volume of water, brought to the boil and 1 oz. of sugar dissolved in this. The bottle is sterilised with boiling water, the prepared orange juice is transferred to the bottle which is immediately closed with a plug of cotton wool which has been sterilised in an oven at medium heat. When the contents of the bottle are quite cool, the agar slant is transferred to the bottle. It is best loosened by a knitting needle which has been dipped into boiling water to ensure that it is sterile. Alternatively a little of the sterile orange juice can be poured into the test tube, the rubber cork is replaced and the contents are well shaken to remove most of the yeast from the agar. This liquid is

77

now transferred to the bottle and in a few days the contents will be in active fermentation and can then be added to the prepared must. If a little of the starter is kept behind in the starter bottle it can be again replenished with sterilised and cooled sweetened orange juice to allow more yeast to grow for other fermentations.

Liquid yeasts are now available in a wide range and are considerably cheaper than tube cultures. They are frequently added direct to the must but in this case the yeast is again not being given a fair chance to dominate the fermentation. However it is possible to avoid producing a starter but yet to allow the yeast to augment sufficiently to make it dominant. This is a particularly useful method as often the must is ready prior to the preparation of the starter. In such a case the must, when properly adjusted with sugar, nutrients and Campden tablets is stored in a refrigerator and only 15 to 20 oz. are transferred to the fermenter. The liquid yeast is added to this small volume of must and the fermenter is put into a warm place. As soon as this must is actively fermenting the rest of the stored must should be warmed to room temperature and then transferred to the fermenter. This method is as effective as if a starter bottle had been prepared but fresh yeast will have to be obtained for further fermentations.

Starter bottles can be stored in the refrigerator till the day before they are wanted and there is no fear that the yeast will degenerate in any way. Nevertheless it will have to be rendered lively, or in other words reactivated, by the addition of a teaspoonful of sugar dissolved in a tablespoonful of boiling water and standing the bottle in a warm place. A lively fermentation will re-ensue in a day or so.

The wine maker who has been in the habit of using baker's yeast will probably be expecting a very violent and foaming fermentation. Such violent fermentations were partly due to the large amounts of baker's yeast which were usually used. It is undesirable for the fermentation to be so vigorous as the yeast becomes exhausted prematurely and the alcohol content will be low. Sometimes fermentation is only evidenced by a ring of bubbles round the surface of the fermenting brew. This, of course, does not apply in the case of a yeast starter when the fermentation should be reasonably vigorous for a few days. The onset of a vigorous fermentation is delayed by cold and speeded up by warm conditions but care must be taken not to have the fermentation too warm as that also spoils the yeast. If the yeast starter is already in full fermentation and wine making has to be delayed there is no harm done. The starter can be kept going by adding one or two teaspoonfuls of sugar dissolved in half a cup of hot water, or the starter can be added to some more sterilized juice in another rather larger bottle. When this is in active fermentation a larger bulk can then be started with this brew or it can all be added to one gallon of juice. The amount of yeast will not be excessive.

CONDUCTING THE FERMENTATION

Adjusting the juice

The production of wine involves a number of stages. First of all the fermenting vessels and the yeast starter have to be got ready. This is then followed by preparing and adjusting the juice. Under this heading comes the washing of the fruit, sterilizing the fruit or fruit juice by heat, the addition of sugar and where necessary of yeast nutrient, acid and Campden tablets.

Whether recipes are used or whether the addition of sugar has been calculated, the juice must be tested for gravity and adjusted again where required before fermentation. The correct technique for fermentation cannot be decided until the type of wine desired has been settled because not only the amount of sugar and the type of yeast but also the way the fermentation is carried out varies. The different wine types have been discussed before and it is not only the composition of the must but the way in which the fermentation and the maturing are carried out which helps to determine their final character. The exact methods of preparation will be fully discussed later.

Fermentation may be carried out on the expressed juice or on the pulp: in the latter case the gravity cannot be taken directly for the purpose of deciding the desirable sugar addition so it is necessary to press a little of the pulp prior to fermentation, strain it through a cloth and to test the juice. While the reading obtained will only give an approximation to the composition of the final juice it will be a good guide. Having made the suitable adjustment the yeast starter, which must be in active fermentation, is added, but the fermentation vessel should not be more than three-quarters full to allow room for frothing. Nevertheless, the vessel should be kept closed with a fermentation trap to protect the wine from contamination but in the case of pulp fermentation it is more convenient to use an open vessel such as a barrel cut in half covered with several layers of cheese cloth tied firmly over it. Once the fermentation has quietened down the fermenter is filled up. The pulp fermentation has, of course, to be treated differently. When sufficient colour is extracted the juice is run off from beneath the top layer, or cap. This is called the 'free run', and makes the best wine. The pulp is then pressed and if it is excessively tart when made from red grapes it may be kept for a poorer wine, but frequently the first pressings are mixed with the free run. When other fruit wines are made by pulp fermentation the free run and the pressings are always mixed and fermented together.

Temperature control

One of the most important influences in wine making is the effect of heat. During fermentation heat is evolved. As over-heating can stop yeast from working particular care must be exercised when the fermenters are large, as the heat developed is less quickly dispersed than from small containers. Also, heat is more readily retained when the juice is covered by a cap of skins or pulped fruit; consequently during commercial red wine production the temperature is checked twice daily to ensure that there is no danger of spoilage. The large fermenters used for pulp fermentation are frequently supplied with cooling devices. As there is less danger from spoilage when fermenting in smaller vessels and as anyhow the prevailing autumn temperature in this country is much lower, the amateur is less likely to encounter spoilage from this source. He may sometimes detect a smell of bad eggs. This is caused by the effect violent fermentation has on the sulphite and this odour will disappear after fermentation, but should it still persist it can be removed by the addition of another Campden tablet to the gallon of the mature wine. By and large the slower the fermentation the better the wine. White wine should be fermented even more slowly than red wine. It is possible to make wines which have a certain amount of sweetness and at the same time a lower alcohol content than is normal for sweet wines. This is brought about by fermenting in the cold, racking while still sweet, encouraging renewed fermentation by bringing the wine into the warm and as soon as this has started the wine is again chilled. The famous Italian Asti Spumanti is made by such complicated methods and the labour involved finds its reward in a wine with a superb flavour. Although fermentation is slowed down by cold this is not really due to the temperature itself so much as to the effect exerted by the retained gas on the yeast. The colder the liquid the more gas will be retained; the warmer it is the more gas is evolved. Yeasts are inhibited to a certain extent by the carbon dioxide gas and this fact is made use of in modern techniques of wine making. The Germans have developed a process known as tank fermentation in which the gas produced by fermentation is partially retained by fermenting in steel tanks which are resistant to pressure. Instead of allowing all the gas to escape during the entire period of fermentation, only a little of the gas is removed at intervals. The fermentation proceeds slowly and results in wines which remain somewhat sweet and yet have the normal alcohol content of white or red table wines. The amateur can also ferment under pressure. If he possesses a Pentacon pressure cooker he can put a stone jar or glass beaker into the cooker, putting his brew into this and replacing the lid. The fermentation is carried out on an adjusted juice with a wine yeast but the vessel and the pressure valve are closed at the start of the fermentation. After a couple of days the pressure valve should be opened to allow excess gas to blow off and this is repeated at intervals. No directions can be given as to the frequency of releasing pressure since it depends on the amount of brew how much gas is evolved. As the amount evolved during a normal fermentation is considerable *it is dangerous* not to release pressure at intervals. Alternatively the valve can be set half open to allow constant evolution of gas but still retain some pressure. The wine maker who gives this method a trial will have to be prepared to experiment and to alter his conditions in subsequent experiments until he arrives at the conditions which give him the wine of the desired quality, but to obtain reproducible results he must always use the same amount of brew in the same-sized pressure vessel.

Sticking fermentations

Just as excess carbon dioxide gas can temporarily inhibit yeast growth, so can heat entirely stop yeast activity. Lack of yeast nutrients in a liquid may also cause the fermentation to cease prematurely. It is always advisable to add yeast nutrient at the start of a fermentation to get a good yeast deposit; adding it once the fermentation has stopped is very seldom effective. New yeast can only grow when there is plenty of oxygen in the juice and fermenting juices will be free from oxygen. If the fermentation sticks then a fresh yeast brew should be made using some of the deposit in the juice. There will be sufficient live yeast there which will become invigorated by being grown in a fresh brew. If it is possible mince a few well-washed apples, add ¼ pint of water and press out the juice. Do not heat this but to ½ pint of juice add 1 tablespoonful of malt extract and 1 ounce of sugar, 1 teaspoonful yeast energizer and some citric acid to make the juice slightly sour. The juice will darken when the yeast energizer is added but acid will soon remove this colour. Add about ¼ pint warm water and then put in a teaspoonful of the yeast from the wine. After a few days this will be in active fermentation and can then be mixed with an equal volume of the sticking wine. As soon as this is fermenting add about twice the amount of wine and so on. It is far more effective to renew fermentation by these means than to add the

19. Small barrel fitted with fermentation lock

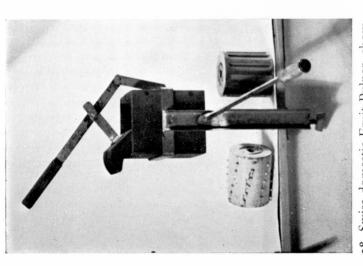

18. Swiss domestic Fruit Pulper, showing components

20. Hydrometers and gravity jar

21. A convenient flask for pulp filtration known as a Valentine flask

yeast brew to the bulk of the sticking wine which will contain some alcohol and other matters inimical to yeast growth. Yeast works best when acclimatized gradually to different environments. It is of course clear that, as everywhere else in wine making, prevention is better, or anyhow less troublesome, than the cure. Sometimes fermentation sticks when the wine has fermented nearly to completion. This is nothing to worry about because slight warming by the sun or by artificial heat will renew the fermentation. Wines sometimes start re-fermenting during the summer and the vintner talks of the wine becoming restless when the vines start to flower in the early summer. This is a sentimental way of looking at it but it is certainly due to the effect of temperature rises and like all life processes rests on sound biological facts. If the spring and summer are warm then no extra heat is required to get the wine to ferment to completion.

Gravity drop during fermentation

It is quite easy to assess how the fermentation is proceeding by testing the juice with a hydrometer at intervals. As the yeast breaks the sugar down into carbon dioxide gas and alcohol so the gravity will drop. This is because sugar has a high gravity and alcohol a low gravity. From the amount by which the gravity has dropped it is possible to assess approximately how much alcohol has been produced. Table VIII gives the relationship between the gravity and the potential alcohol, that is, the alcohol which will be produced when all the sugar has been converted and the wine is dry. From this it will be seen that comparatively less alcohol is formed when the sugar content is low. The reason for this is that the yeasts use up some of the sugar for yeast growth and this is more apparent when gravities are low.

Racking

Wines are not generally racked till the fermentation has almost ceased but when wines are made commercially the vintner often exercises a measure of control over the quality of his wine by

TABLE VIII

COMPARISON BETWEEN THE SPECIFIC GRAVITY OF A GRAPE JUICE AND THE POTENTIAL ALCOHOL LIKELY TO BE FORMED

This table is not applicable to the fermentation of fruit juices other than grapes because in the case of most other fruits available in Britain considerable additions of syrup (or water and sugar) are usually made. This dilutes the non-sugar solids and consequently higher alcohol levels are attained than when pure grape juice is fermented.

A considerable amount of research on this matter has proved that dividing the gravity drop occurring during fermentation by the factor 7·36 gives the percentage alcohol by volume present almost identically with that found by the usual analytical technique of distillation, which of course requires special apparatus and some skill.

Specific Gravity	Gravity	Percentage potential alcohol (by vol.)
1·030	30	2·9
1·035	35	3·6
1·037	37	4·0
1·040	40	4·6
1·045	45	5·3
1·050	50	6·0
1·052	52	6·3
1·055	55	6·8
1·060	60	7·6
1·065	65	8·4
1·067	67	8·7
1·070	70	9·2
1·075	75	10·0
1·080	80	10·8
1·083	83	11·2
1·085	85	11·5
1·090	90	12·3
1·095	95	13·1
1·100	100	13·6
1·110	110	14·8
1·120	120	16·0
1·130	130	17·2
1·140	140	18·4
1·150	150	19·5

racking earlier. This is frequently carried out while there is still a small amount of sugar present even on wines which are intended to become dry. Sometimes racking is undertaken during the primary fermentation, especially when the fermentation is too vigorous. This premature racking is somewhat dangerous in the hands of amateurs and often leads to sticking and lack of clarification. In general wines should only be racked when they begin to clarify, that is when the yeast has started to settle.

DETERMINATION OF THE ALCOHOL CONTENT OF A WINE

Naturally most winemakers would like to know the alcohol content of their wines but unfortunately there are no very simple methods of determining this as the slightest trace of sugar left in the wine at the end of fermentation will make any direct test inaccurate.

The chemist determines the alcohol by distilling it off from a measured quantity of the wine in a special glass apparatus, making up to a known volume with water and determining the specific gravity by weighing a known volume at a correct temperature from which the alcohol content can be determined from tables. For this type of work a hydrometer is not usually accurate enough.

A simpler method is to take say 200 ml. of the wine, put it in an open porcelain evaporating dish, drive off the alcohol by boiling gently for a little while and when cool make up the residual liquid to 200 ml. again and take the gravity with a hydrometer. This will be higher than the original gravity of the wine because of the loss of alcohol. Alcohol is lighter than water and so lowers the gravity of an alcohol-water mixture such as wine. Determine this increase in gravity and subtract from 1.000 and look up the resulting figure in Table IX to determine the percentage of alcohol present.

For example, if the sp. gr. of the wine was 1·012 (gravity = 12) and after removing the alcohol this became 1·025, the difference is ·013; subtract from 1·000 = 0·987 = 9·65 % alcohol by volume. But it is easy to make small errors when taking readings with a hydrometer. Suppose the correct figure should have been 0·9875, which is only a very small error, but reference to the tables shows that the alcohol content would then have been 9·22%. In other words it is unlikely that results by this method will be accurate within ½%.

TABLE IX

ALCOHOL TABLE

Specific Gravity at 60° F.	Alcohol by Volume	Percent Proof Spirit
0·9928	5·03	8·77
0·9915	6·01	10·49
0·9902	7·02	12·25
0·9889	8·06	14·08
0·9877	9·05	15·82
0·9865	10·08	17·59
0·9854	11·04	19·25
0·9843	12·02	20·97
0·9832	13·02	22·71
0·9821	14·04	24·50
0·9810	15·08	26·32
0·9800	16·04	27·99
0·9790	17·01	29·70
0·9780	18·00	31·42
0·9769	19·09	33·31
0·9759	20·08	35·04
0·9749	21·07	36·79
0·9739	22·06	38·52
0·9729	23·04	40·24
0·9719	24·01	41·94

These figures show that a very accurate hydrometer is needed which reads to 4 places and of course the alcohol must be tested at 60°F. with a hydrometer which is calibrated to read at that temperature.

Another method, and the most suitable one for most purposes, is to determine the gravity of the juice before fermentation is allowed to start and subtract from this the gravity of the finished wine (making allowances if necessary for any liquid added during the fermentation). Divide this figure by 7·36 to obtain the alcohol content by volume.

Say the gravity was 135 to start with and 20 at the finish. Difference 115 divide by 7·36 = 15·6%.

TABLE X

ALCOHOL CONTENT CALCULATED FROM THE DROP OF
GRAVITY

Gravity Drop	Alcohol by Volume
80	10·9
90	12·2
100	13·6
110	14·9
120	16·3
130	17·7
140	19·0
150	20·3
160	21·6
170	23·0

When the sugar is added in stages during the fermentation the true original gravity of the juice is not known, but, provided the sugar is added in the form of syrup, it can be calculated if the gravity is taken before and after each sugar addition and the volumes are also known.

Suppose fermentation was started with 1 gallon of fruit juice of gravity of 80 and this was fermented down to 20 when 55 oz. of syrup was added and the gravity rose to 90. The initial gravity of 80 of the 160 oz. of juice would be effectively reduced by the increase in volume so that it would be $80 \times \frac{160}{215} = 60$. To this add the increase in gravity $90 - 20 = 70$. Hence the true original gravity on which any calculation must be based is $60 + 70 = 130$.

CLARIFICATION AND MATURING

Natural clarification

Wine if properly made should clarify naturally. Storing the wine in the cold is a great help in inducing clarification. Sometimes a certain amount of clarification can be brought about by stirring up the yeast deposit which has formed after the first racking and delaying the second racking till the yeast has settled again. Cold also assists in removing cream of tartar which settles out as hard, glass-like crystals in wines made from grapes.

Clarification by added fining agents

If the wine does not clarify of its own accord then fining must be resorted to after the second or third racking. Fining is achieved by forming in the wine by some convenient means a loose textured insoluble precipitate which settles relatively slowly and in doing so attracts other insoluble matter which will then settle with it.

Fining used to be an extremely difficult operation and not one that could be carried out with any measure of success by amateurs. All sorts of finings were used: isinglass, casein, agar, gelatin together with tannin, white of egg and even milk. Most of these finings, and particularly isinglass, are very tricky to handle and may easily lead to worse and completely persistent hazes. A new fining has now been developed which does not suffer from the real disadvantages of those hitherto available. These finings, called Serena Wine Finings,[1] consist of a packet the contents of which have to be dissolved in water, and known as Finings A, and a liquid in a bottle known as Finings B. One or two teaspoonfuls of each is added to a gallon of wine when they will interact to form an insoluble deposit and in the course of settling will entrain the clouding matter in the wine. For most wines the above quantity is all that is needed but there are a few wines which are very thick, due to too much pectin, when even the most effective finings may fail. In these cases one tablespoonful of a pectin-destroying enzyme[1] should be added to the wine which should be kept in a warm place between 75° and 80°F for a few days till the wine has become thin. After this it must be fined. If the fining has been carried out in a barrel and if, after settling, the liquid runs off clear it can then be transferred directly into bottles until very little is left behind. The remainder will have to be filtered. The best way to filter is to use a quick filtering paper, Fords No. 541, as the inner filtering surface and Fords No. 5 as the outer paper, folding

[1] Obtainable from Grey Owl Laboratories Ltd., Kingswood, Bristol.

the two together and inserting into a funnel. If the fining has been done in a glass vessel the clear liquid should be syphoned off through a rubber tube into a clean container prior to bottling. The dregs must again be filtered.

Filtration through Pulp

Another method of clarifying which is particularly satisfactory is by filtering the wine through asbestos pulp. Many vintners prefer this method to fining. It is carried out by beating a handful of pulp for say five gallons or so, a little less for a gallon, in a jug with some water. Take a glass funnel or a Valentine's Flask (see plate 21) which has been loosely plugged with some cotton wool, rest the weight of a tablespoon on this cotton wool to hold the plug down, pour the asbestos-water mixture onto this and do not remove the spoon from the funnel nor let the asbestos drain dry but pour more water over this until the liquid is free from the taste of asbestos. Then carry on by pouring the cloudy wine gently onto the asbestos. If it does not come through clear, pour back through the asbestos until it does clear. Continue until the whole of the wine is clear. This method of clarifying is quicker than filtration through filter paper but is still too slow to be suitable for large volumes of wine. In such cases Serena Finings are more practical and less damaging to the wine as there is less exposure to air. In commercial production wines are fined and then passed through filter presses.

Filtration through Filter Paper

If the wine is clear the bulk of it can be drawn off and bottled but the residue or lees must be filtered. It is preferable to use two filter papers of different fineness. No. 541 Whatman is quick filtering but does not filter brilliantly clear, while No. 5 is slow but gives a perfectly clear wine. The filter papers are placed together, No. 541 on top so that it will be inside and the papers are then folded in half and then in half again to make a quarter. The flaps are then folded back on to the fold, then once more back on themselves so that these portions are a sixteenth of the whole while the centre piece is an eighth. Holding the folded flaps, the paper is opened to the original quarter and the flaps are folded inwards towards the inside of the fold. The cone is then bent back at the original quarter fold so as to bring the fold outwards. The folded papers are then opened out and a perfect fluted filter cone is the result. A little practice or a demonstration from a chemist will soon enable the vintner to achieve this.

The No. 541 paper which is on the inside will serve to filter out the coarser particles and prevent the No. 5 paper from getting clogged and becoming unduly slow. The cone is placed on a little cushion of cotton wool inside a funnel. This helps to protect the point and prevents it from breaking. During the folding, care must be taken not to press the folds down to the point, as that would put an undue strain on the paper. The idea of fluting the paper is to present a large surface for filtration and thus to speed up the output

Maturing

The young wine may taste very unpleasant and the most important stage of wine production starts now. It is here where the wine maker must learn to exercise his judgment. At the first racking the wine will taste raw and unpleasant and may be hazy. After another month or so the wine will be much clearer and taste already better. The containers must be kept full at all costs and if there are no small quantities left over for filling up, then the wine must be transferred to a smaller vessel. Some commercial vintners will even fill up with water rather than have any air space in the barrel. After another two or three months the wine is racked again. If the wine is a dry one it must be tested for what is called 'bottle ripeness'. First of all some is put into a glass and stood in the open for a few days. It must not darken, or if it does then the wine has to be sulphited again with one tablet to the gallon and re-tested. Another portion is transferred to a bottle, which is filled three-quarters full and corked. The wine is stood in a warm place for a week. It should not throw a deposit nor form bubbles round the perimeter of the liquid nor should the cork blow out. If any of these things happen then the wine is not yet ready for bottling.

If the wine passes these tests it is still desirable to add one or two *Reductone Tablets*[1] per gallon to ensure that it remains in a fully reduced state which means that it will retain its fresh flavour and not develop off flavours. This is desirable even if sulphite had to be added as above to prevent darkening. The same result could be obtained by adding excess sulphite but this adds a distinct and undesirable flavour to the wine which should be avoided.

Sweet wines and very tart wines have to undergo prolonged periods of maturing and are best matured in wood with regular racking at three-or four-monthly intervals. Also both sulphite and Reductone Tablets have to be added as needed, both to prevent darkening and to keep the flavour fresh. The necessity in the case of sweet wines is rather greater than for dry but can only be assessed by tasting and testing through standing in an open glass. Sufficient sulphite to prevent browning in an open glass should be added before the Reductone Tablets are added. It is much easier to prevent darkening than to remove any brown colour formed. In the latter case sulphite alone does not suffice but the wine has to be decolorized with charcoal.

Blending, adjusting acidity and taste

Here again, experience will assist the wine maker to produce a more palatable wine. Sometimes a wine turns out rather too sweet while another is much too sharp. Small, but known quantities can be mixed in a measuring cylinder and the wine then tasted. If, for instance, it requires 10 mil. of wine A and 15 mil. of wine B to produce a palatable mixture then this means that the wine should be blended in the proportion of 1 to 1½ or 2 to 3. *After blending, wines must undergo at least a few weeks of storage in bulk before bottling to ensure that fermentation does not re-ensue.* Sometimes acid has to be added to the wine as this helps to bring out the flavour, or it may

[1] Obtainable from Grey Owl Laboratories Ltd., Kingswood Bristol.

be too sharp when some acid will need removing by the addition of chalk. If the wine tastes insipid the addition of some grape tannin will markedly improve the flavour. The amount which has to be added can only be decided by the method of trial and error, but this skill is one soon acquired by wine makers keen to produce a quality wine. Some acid wines can be made to become less sour by delaying racking, stirring up the yeast deposit and bringing the wine into the warm. Acid-reducing bacteria will become active under these conditions and by their acid-reducing action render the wine less sour and vastly improve its quality. If the wine, though, is excessively sour these bacteria are inhibited. A slight reduction by chalk, say $\frac{1}{4}$—$\frac{1}{2}$ oz. per gallon, will reduce the acid to such a level that by delaying racking and applying warmth the acid-reducing bacteria can then complete the job and render the wine less acid. This is better than using too much chalk (see also page 60).

Bottling

The vintner who has carried out his fermentation properly and with a sedimentary yeast will now be able to see the results of his care. His wine should be clear and he should be able to draw off into bottles through the tap or by syphoning off through a ubber tube. If there is *no* yeast deposit then the wine can be poured into a jug and bottles filled by pouring through a glass or plastic funnel. Before bottling, however, he should make sure that one or two Reductone Tablets (see page 91) per gallon have been added to the wine as these will ensure that it will remain sound and of good flavour.

The bottles should be well washed with a detergent and rinsed out with some sulphite solution. This can be prepared from Campden tablets by dissolving ten tablets in half a pint of water and using this to rinse the bottles. They must be allowed to drain for half an hour or else be given a light rinse before filling to avoid too much sulphite being added to the wine. The bottles should be corked immediately they are filled. New corks should be used and straight-sided corks are the best to choose. The corks are softened for a few hours in hot water to which some sulphite should be added. They are then rinsed and well drained shortly before being required and are finally hammered home with a mallet. The filled bottles must stand in a dry room for a day so as to dry the corks and then they are preferably capped with a lead capsule as this helps to hold the cork in position. Failing that, the cork can be wired or tied down.

Storing

The bottles must be stored lying flat. This prevents the cork from drying out as in such a case the wine would tend to spoil through air penetrating the cork. If the wine has been properly matured corks should not blow out, but beginners are advised to inspect their bottles occasionally. If a very slight creamy deposit is noted along the wall of the bottle then this is due to yeast and may lead to renewed fermentation. In the case of fortified red wines such as Port, a dark-coloured deposit may not be due to yeast but to red colouring matter being thrown out. This deposit is called a crust and crusted ports are very much appreciated by the connoisseur. To prevent the crust from being disturbed through inadvertently turning the bottle, each is marked by a spot of paint on the top. When the bottle is to be opened the spot of paint indicates how to hold the bottle. The wine has to be carefully decanted from the bottle without disturbing this crust (see page 23).

WINE DISEASES AND THEIR PREVENTION

No book on wine making would be complete without reference to spoilage. Wine spoilage is entirely preventable when small quantities are made by proper methods as it is possible to ensure cleanliness of fruit and to prevent vinegar formation through fruit flies. In large scale production such care cannot always be exercised and spoilage is more likely. Spoilage is always easier to prevent than to cure and the wine maker should be aware of the dangers so that he can avoid them.

Vinegar formation

First and foremost in wine diseases is *Acetification*, or vinegar formation. Vinegar bacteria are found in damaged fruit and in honey, and are introduced by the little fruit flies which are always found hovering around decaying fruit or spilled wine. The bacteria thrive under certain conditions. First of all they require air or oxygen and a weak alcohol solution which they convert into vinegar. By preventing access of fruit flies, by boiling fruit which has gone overripe, by using sulphite where boiling is not convenient, by fermenting to a sufficiently high alcohol strength and by keeping containers *full* once the primary fermentation is over vinegar formation can be prevented. There is no remedy once much vinegar is present. If the wine maker tastes his brew at intervals he can prevent excessive acetification. At the slightest sign of vinegar formation the wine must be sulphited and re-fermented with some fresh pulp. If much vinegar has formed the only thing to do is to let the wine turn completely and when it has finished its transformation, bottle it and pasteurize the bottles to preserve the vinegar. Wine vinegar or fruit vinegar is much appreciated for culinary purposes. Pasteurizing is carried out by standing the bottles in water, heating this till it attains 140° F., keeping it at this temperature for 20 minutes and corking the bottles before cooling.

Flowers of Wine

This disease is due to a yeast-like body called mycoderma. This forms on the surface of the wine at first as little white flecks which eventually coalesce to a white wrinkled skin. This skin is similar in appearance, but not in colour, to that which may be formed by a sherry yeast. Sherry films are creamy in colour and tend to go brown and are due to a particular film-forming yeast which likes to live on the surface of a wine. Sherry films are much tougher than mycoderma films which break easily. Unlike sherry yeast, my-coderma will break a wine down to carbon dioxide and water. As soon as the flecks appear the wine should be given another dose of sulphite and filtered at once into bottles or other non-wooden containers which must be filled to the top. Once a thick film has formed the wine is spoilt.

Oiliness

Sometimes wines go thick and appear oily on pouring. This disorder is of bacterial origin. The wine can be made drinkable by beating the wine into a froth and sulphiting with two Campden tablets per gallon. This must be followed by filtration through pulp or paper.

White, Brown and Black Break

The word 'break' is a translation of the French word *casse* which is literally translated as 'break' but which can also be interpreted as 'spoilage'. The wine develops white or coloured hazes which are due to metallic contaminations such as traces of copper, iron or zinc. This shows the importance of using glass, stoneware or wood containers and taking care that only sound enamel saucepans are used. (Aluminium frequently affects the colouring matter in a wine and aluminium pans are therefore not used.) The addition of some citric acid will generally remove discoloration due to iron or copper.

Bitterness

This is due mainly to unsuitable yeast and lack of acidity during the fermentation. It must be avoided as there is little cure for it; it can occur in red wines due to mouldy grapes.

Darkening and consequent Off Flavours

Again, these are better prevented than cured. Both fining with milk and treatment with charcoal will render white wines paler.

For 10 gallons mix 2 oz. of a good decolorizing carbon and ½ oz. of a 10 per cent potassium bisulphite solution with a little wine and stir this into the bulk of the wine. If the carbon is fairly coarse this should settle after a while. If not the wine must be filtered.

This comprehensive list of wine diseases should not cause any apprehension to the wine maker. If he is careful to protect his wines from air, to use clean fruit, pure yeast cultures and wooden, stone or glass containers none of the diseases are at all likely to occur.

$\{4\}$

The Production of Different Wine Types

DETAILED PROCEDURE OF WINE MAKING

Fermenting for different Wine Types

Reference has already been made to the fact that wines not only differ in flavour and appearance but that they are made by different methods. These methods must be studied and some consideration given to them when trying to make different wine types.

What constitutes these differences? It is partly due to the amount of sugar present at the start of the fermentation and partly to the treatment meted out to the yeasts and the conditions under which fermentation is carried out. Roughly, wines can be divided into five classes.

(1) *Dry White Table Wines.*

(2) *Dry Red Table Wines.* These two are produced from juices of low gravity with plenty of natural yeast nutrients present. Generally the fermentation is quick.

(3) *Sweet Dessert Wines.* These come from juices low in natural yeast nutrients and high in initial sugar content. Fermentation is therefore sluggish but this results in good flavours.

(4) *Sparkling Wines.* These are wines which undergo a renewed fermentation in bottles or closed containers. The wines are first fermented to dryness and allowed to clarify. They are then blended with some syrup, a champagne yeast and extra yeast nutrients. When this blend starts to ferment it is at once bottled in heavy champagne bottles, the corks wired down and the bottles

97

stored for at least nine months in the cold. The wine should be dry and clear at the end of this time. The yeast is removed by bringing it down on to the corks through gradually inverting the bottles. The removal of the yeast is called disgorging, and is done by putting the neck of the bottle into a freezing mixture or solid carbon dioxide, which causes the contents in the neck to freeze solid. The bottles are then held upright and the wire is cut. The cork, with its frozen plug of wine and yeast, is blown out by the pressure in the bottle and the vintner, who has to work extremely quickly, puts his little finger round the inside of the neck to remove any adherent yeast. The bottle is then quickly filled up with a 'Dose', a liquor containing sugar and alcohol which enables the champagne to be sweetened to the desired extent. The bottle is generally filled up and corked in a special machine and it is not possible for an amateur to cork his bottles with champagne corks. He is best served by making his champagne in stout cider flagons or beer bottles which are closed by rubber-covered screw stoppers or by using plastic stoppers.

(5) *Fortified Wines*. These are wines which have been strengthened by the addition of alcohol; two types of fortified wines exist: the Sherry type and the sweet fortified red and tawny wines such as Malaga, Madeira, Marsala, Tarragona and red and white Port. The latter are generally fortified while they still contain some sugar, in the case of Port as much as 9 per cent sugar. Port and Tarragona are produced from red grapes, with the exception of white port, while the other fortified wines are all made from white grapes. They are rendered dark and sweet by the addition of grape concentrate; this results in full-bodied, deeply coloured, rich sweet wines. They are matured in full containers and not exposed to the air more than necessary, but are racked at intervals and if any sign of renewed fermentation is noted more grape spirit is added. The high alcohol content makes them very costly to English consumers mainly on account of the high rate of duty applied by the Commissioners of Excise.

Port wine cannot be made without fortification and any wine made by fermenting to dryness or even to near dryness will be

23. Red Hybrid Vine. Seibel 5455. Early ripening and prolific

22. Red European Vine. Black Hamburgh. Almondsbury Vineyard. Late ripening

25. Vines growing over trees in Portugal

24. Vines grown for Vinho Verde trained on granite posts in Portugal

thin in body when compared with port. Also there are not many indigenous fruits available for port wine making. Damsons are probably the best for colour but the juice must be rendered less tart. Bilberries can be made into a wine resembling port very closely, but this fruit is difficult to come by in large enough quantities. Elderberries are rather too bitter. The best way is to use a red, small-berried grape, fermenting the juice to as high an alcohol content as possible and then adding some red grape concentrate which can either be purchased or made by boiling some red grapes, pressing, partly removing the acid by chalk, filtering and concentrating the juice by heating. When most of the alcohol is produced by the fermentation then a comparatively small amount of fortification can be carried out and will prove less costly than if the fermentation had been stopped by alcohol and the greater part of the alcohol present had to be added as is done in Portugal (see also page 119).

A different type of fortification is practised in the case of Sherry. This wine is produced from very sweet white grapes, the juice of which is allowed to ferment to completion. It will probably contain a little sugar and if the alcohol content is less than 16–17 per cent it is fortified to that level to prevent acetification. The wine is stored in barrels four-fifths full, and after a while a film may form. The wine is transferred to a solera where the blending is carried out progressively. This was outlined on page 18. Obviously the amateur wine maker cannot make sherry by such methods, nor is it at all necessary, but it is useful to know how sherry is produced commercially. It is obvious that the difference between a sherry and an ordinary wine is that in normal wine production the wine is kept pale and free from oxidation by all air being excluded. For sherry air is admitted freely and the sherry can consequently become golden or darker in colour. Hence, if a fruit juice, such as that of apples, blackberries or plums, is fermented in air then a sherry-like quality will ensue. All Spanish sherries are at first fermented to dryness and if required sweet they are sweetened with grape concentrate, that is a grape juice which has been boiled till it is dark and syrupy. The amateur wine maker can use concentrated apple juice or grape juice but it is important that some of the acid be removed prior to concentrating by boiling down in an open pan. Alternatively he can use some golden syrup to sweeten his sherry, or he can ferment a high gravity juice which contains too much sugar to go dry. Provided the juice is 'clean' there is very little danger of acetification. If a sherry yeast has been used, provided the temperature is right (about 70° Fahrenheit) and the wine contains about 2½ per cent of sugar, then a sherry film may form and produce a particularly fine sherry flavour. Wines under a sherry film will go pale and thus become Fino sherries. Oloroso are sweet dark sherries which have not fermented under a film. Despite the studies that have been carried out on sherry production there does not seem to be any certainty how a sherry will mature or whether it will form a film. The vintner allows the fermentation to take its course but he classifies his sherries prior to maturing and blending.

The foregoing shows that there is a good deal of control and adjustment required in sherry making but the amateur need only ensure that plenty of air gets at his wine both during or after the fermentation for the achievement of sherry quality. The wine must, of course, be protected from vinegar flies and this is best done by using a fermentation trap without the water which seals off the air, and plugging the opening of the trap with a little cotton wool. Furthermore, the wine should only be racked once at completion of primary fermentation and is subsequently left on its yeast deposit.

PRODUCTION OF DRY WHITE WINE FROM GRAPES

It depends on the size of the vintage whether or not a yeast starter is first prepared. For instance, if it is intended to make at once from five to ten gallons of wine, then a starter must be prepared. On the other hand, if it is possible to make the wine in stages starting with one gallon, then a liquid culture or a tube culture can be added direct to the must.

Should a starter be decided upon, then a few days before picking the grapes a few bunches of the ripest grapes should be collected from the vineyard and the juice pressed out. This juice is used for a yeast starter. By the time the grapes are picked the yeast starter should be in full and active fermentation. If for some reason or other the onset of the vintage has to be delayed then the fermentation in the starter can be kept in an active state by adding a teaspoonful of sugar at intervals. The duration of these intervals depends on the rate at which renewed fermentation becomes apparent and it is only after the peak of the fermentation has been passed that more sugar should be added.

It is desirable to pick the fruit when it is dry and to cut out any vinegar sour or mouldy berries,[1] although a very small amount of mould will not do much harm if more sulphite is added to the mouldy juice than to one which is produced from sound berries. The stems are first removed and the fruit is crushed by hand by pounding with a potato masher or by a suitable crusher. The pulp is placed in a coarse hessian bag and pressed. Pressing is carried out gradually as too much initial pressure is only likely to damage the fabric and the fruit press and will not yield more juice. As the juice runs out the pulp becomes drier and finally will be compressed into quite a hard pad. Nevertheless the pulp will still contain some juice and there is no reason why the pulp from 14 lb. of grapes should not be mixed with about a pint of water and re-pressed. The wine maker will wish to know the yield he can obtain from his grapes. The greater the bulk that is made the less wastage there will be and it is possible to make 10 gallons of wine from 120–130 lb. of grapes. If making smaller quantities one can reckon from 3–4 lb. of grapes to fill a 26 oz. bottle; this is the normal size in which English wines are marketed and is called the reputed quart.

The juice must next be tested for gravity and preferably also for acidity. For a delicate dry white wine it is generally considered

[1] Outdoor grapes do not ripen sufficiently in this country for the mould to prove beneficial. Greenhouse grapes can frequently be used mouldy. If drops of golden and very sweet juice are seen exuding on mouldy berries then the mould is beneficial or 'ennobling' to wine quality.

that a gravity of 90 is the best starting point but most outdoor grapes grown in this country will have a lower gravity than this, probably between 50 and 70 so they will need some added sugar. This is because grapes seldom become fully ripe under our climatic conditions and for the same reason the juice is usually somewhat acid. Of course, greenhouse grapes should contain more sugar and less acid.

The acidity can be determined quite simply by titration as explained on page 181 but if this is not convenient it can be assumed that the acidity of the juice of ripe outdoor grapes will be at least 1·25 per cent. To get a good wine this should preferably be reduced to about 1 per cent and this can be done quite simply at the same time as adjusting the sugar concentration by the addition of syrup which will increase the volume of the juice and so reduce its acidity. First let us consider the volume of syrup to add and later what strength the syrup should be.

If the acidity is above 1¼ per cent but below 1½ per cent the juice will have to be diluted by the addition of one gallon of syrup to four gallons of juice. If the acidity ranges between 1½ per cent and 2 per cent then one gallon of syrup has to be added to each three gallons of juice.

From the gravity of the juice and the quantity of syrup which is going to be added to it, it is possible to calculate the concentration or the gravity of the syrup which should be used but to avoid a complex calculation the following figures can be used and will apply to most juices:

Initial gravity of grape juice	Addition of 1 gallon syrup to 4 gallons juice. Required gravity of syrup to produce a final gravity of		Addition of 1 gallon syrup to 3 gallons juice. Required gravity of syrup to produce a final gravity of	
	90	100	90	100
50	250	300	210	250
60	210	260	180	220
70	170	220	150	190
80	130	180	120	160
90	90	140	90	130
100	50	100	60	100

The proportions of sugar and water required to make syrups of these various gravities are given in Table VII on page 72.

Should the acidity of the juice be above 2 per cent then $\frac{1}{2}$ per cent of the acid should be removed by the addition of chalk as explained on page 60.

Having adjusted the juice to the most desirable gravity and acidity it should preferably be sulphited by the addition of one Campden tablet to each gallon, or if the grapes were unsound double this amount is required. The Campden tablets are broken up and dissolved in a cup with a little of the juice to make sure that it is evenly distributed throughout the juice. This is followed by the addition of a starter which has been prepared as outlined on page 77 and a little yeast nutrient, particularly if syrup had been added. The juice can either be transferred to a barrel or left in a wide-mouthed tub which can be covered with a lid and a cloth to prevent access of fruit flies, but it should not be left for more than a few days. If the juice is at once placed in a barrel a head space amounting to about one-tenth the capacity of the barrel must be left; in other words, no more than 9 gallons of juice should be placed into a 10 gallon barrel. If the juice has been left in the tub and care taken to protect it, nevertheless the wine must be drawn off into barrels before the start of the secondary fermentation. If the weather is very warm the primary fermentation may be complete in as little as two or three days but such rapid fermentation does not give fine quality wines so sometimes fermentation is slowed down by racking to remove some of the yeast or by chilling.

Vintners who delay the vintage till November are frequently rewarded by having wines with much improved flavours and this is partly due to the incidence of cold weather during the period of the primary fermentation. It is usual to follow the drop in gravity by testing the juice daily with a hydrometer and if the drop amounts to 10 degrees per day then a gravity of 10 will be reached in about eight to nine days. At this gravity the juice should be drawn off into barrels and allowed to complete the secondary fermentation in these containers. The barrels must be filled to the top during the secondary fermentation and kept full till the wine is ready for bottling. This shows the need for arranging the amount which is to be fermented so that there is more juice than will fill a fermenter. If 5 gallons have been made to start with then the most suitable barrel to use is a pin which has a capacity of 4½ gallons. Sometimes when 10 gallons have been made it may be necessary to draw off into two 4½ gallon containers if there is not sufficient wine to fill up the 10 gallon barrel. There are always losses in wine making, partly by evaporation but partly by the space which is occupied by the yeast deposit. When drawing off from this at racking time the volume drawn off is always less than the original volume. The wine will carry on a slow secondary fermentation during the winter and if it is desired to bottle a wine without maturing then the secondary fermentation must be brought to completion by warming the wine. On the other hand many vintners will let their wine rest in barrels during the summer when the fermentation will complete owing to the warmer weather. Wines are racked about three times a year and during this racking they should clarify. Sometimes, though, a wine will not clarify without a little assistance and stirring up the yeast deposit may be all that is necessary to bring about clarification; if not, fining must be resorted to as described on page 88. When wine is made from grapes a certain amount of the acid is made insoluble through the action of the alcohol and this acid will deposit on the sides and bottom of the barrel during the cold weather. These crystals are called cream of tartar and are used quite extensively as a raising agent in the baking industry. The crystals may dissolve to a slight extent on warming and it is therefore important to rack the wine which has undergone a period of cold before the weather turns warm. Unless this is done the vintner may find needle-like crystals of cream of tartar coming out in his bottled wine. Dry white wines should be protected from the effects of air as much as possible and are preferably bottled and drunk young. Immediately after bottling the wine may suffer from off flavours called bottle-sickness. This is a temporary malaise and is mainly due to the effect of air and will disappear on storage. Bottles are always stored lying on their sides to keep the corks moist to avoid shrinkage, thus preventing air getting into the wine.

The following example shows the adjustment required and the kind of fermentation which may be expected. When the juice was first tested its gravity was found to be 58. The sugar content was about 12 per cent and the acid content just over 1 per cent. It is obvious that this juice would require some dilution and some sugar addition. It was therefore decided to add 10 per cent of syrup of gravity 300. That is, to 15 gallons of juice 1½ gallons of syrup were added to make 16½ gallons. To calculate the resulting gravity is easy.

Multiply the gravity of the
juice by its volume, i.e.
$58 \times 15 =$ 870

Multiply the gravity of syrup
by its volume, i.e. $300 \times 1 \cdot 5 =$ 450
                                                  ─────
Add   1320

                                                  1320
Divide total by total volume   ──── = 80
                                                  16·5

The juice therefore will have a gravity of 80 and this from Table III will give about 10·8 per cent of alcohol by volume.

Just as the addition of syrup has increased the sugar content so the acid content will have become reduced by the dilution in a similar proportion, i.e. 15 gallons have been increased to 16½ gallons, therefore the acid has been reduced by $\frac{15}{16 \cdot 5}$, i.e. 1 per cent has become 0·9 per cent. It would have been possible to reduce the acid even more by adding a greater quantity of a weaker syrup but this makes the wine thin and it is better to add a little chalk to remove some of the acid. ¼ oz. of chalk to the gallon removes about ¼ per cent of acid and that would bring the acidity down to 0·65 per cent. Acid removal is best carried out on the juice rather than on the finished wine.

As fruit juices low in sugar ferment rather quickly it was

decided not to add the syrup at first as the amount of sugar which would have been added would not have been sufficient to slow the fermentation. Fermenting the fruit juice first and then racking from most of the yeast prior to adding syrup had the advantage that the fermentation after racking was much slower. The usual addition of yeast culture and 1 teaspoonful of yeast nutrient was made. The gravity of the juice which was 58 on October 9th dropped to 9 by October 15th. This was then racked, the syrup added and well mixed whereupon the 16½ gallons were transferred into a 12 gallon cask and a 4½ gallon pin and left undisturbed. By January 1st the wine had cleared and had a gravity of 0·994. It was racked into a clean barrel and 1 Campden tablet added for each 2 gallons of juice. After 2 months the wine was tasted and a little stood in an open glass for 2 days. It did not darken. Another portion was put into a white bottle which was corked and stood in a warm place for a week. No sediment was noted nor was pressure developed in the bottle. Hence the wine was ready for bottling. If it had darkened, then some more sulphite would have had to be added. If it had thrown a sediment, then the wine would have required a second racking and leaving for another two months before testing and bottling. This wine was actually a little low in tannin and 1 tablespoonful of grape tannin was added to the 16½ gallons of wine. The amount was arrived at by trial and error, stirring in a strong solution made by adding 1 tablespoonful to a cup of hot water and adding this little by little to the wine, stirring and tasting.

The next example demonstrates a fermentation which also progressed slowly and satisfactorily to completion. The wine was made from imported Greek grapes which were of the thin-skinned variety also known as water grapes. The gravity of the juice from these grapes was again low, i.e. 58 and here again the juice was fermented by itself at first and then syrup was added. The addition of syrup cheapens the wine and it is possible to make just over a gallon of wine at a total cost of 10s. od. provided the grapes are bought wholesale. That works out at 1s. 6d. a bottle. The gravity drops show how quickly the primary fermentation was completed and how subsequent addition of syrup improved the fermentation by slowing it down.

Date	Gravity
Sept. 2	58
4	48
7	12

Here syrup was added to bring the gravity up to 48. Also 1 teaspoonful of yeast nutrient was added together with the syrup. The amount of syrup used was 1 pint and it is quite easy to calculate the gravity which will be obtained when 7 pints of brew (i.e. it was neither juice nor wine as it was still fermenting) of gravity 12 is mixed with 1 pint of syrup of gravity 300.

$$7 \times 12 = 84$$
$$1 \times 300 = \underline{300}$$
$$384$$

Divide the total by 8 = 48

1 pint is a suitable amount of syrup to add because it would have brought the original gravity up to 88 if it had been added prior to fermentation. This is calculated as follows:

$$7 \text{ pints} \times 58 = 406$$
$$1 \text{ pint} \times 300 = \underline{300}$$
$$706$$

Divide the total by 8 = 88

Syrup addition took place on September 7th and the gravity was 48. By the 10th it had dropped to 34 and to nil by the 18th of September and to ·995 on the 27th September.

Date	Gravity
Sept. 7	48
10	34
18	0
27	0·995 i.e. below 1·0 Sp. Gr. (see page 40)

This wine was very good in flavour and although dry was most palatable.

From the foregoing it is seen that adding syrup is a very satisfactory way of producing a wine from grapes low in sugar. This is done very extensively in German wine production and dry sugar is only used for juices which are low in acid.

THE PRODUCTION OF DRY RED WINE FROM GRAPES

The red colouring matter of grapes is almost entirely present in the skin. There are some grapes the juice of which also is red but the colour is quite insufficient to produce red wine. Red pigments can be extracted from the skins to a certain extent by heating the pulp but a better and more convenient method is to carry out the fermentation in the presence of the skins. The alcohol which is formed during fermentation will leach out the colour and the more alcohol that is present the darker will the wine become. It is therefore desirable to add sugar or syrup to the pulp prior to fermentation, anyhow to grapes low in sugar, so as to ensure good colour extraction by the alcohol which is formed. These types of wines are preferred with an alcohol content of 10 per cent to 12 per cent, so an initial gravity of from 85 to 100 is desirable. As the stems of the grapes contain much tannin it is absolutely essential that they be removed prior to pulping the fruit. The pulp should be mixed with the required amount of syrup and from 1 to 2 Campden tablets per 10 lb. of fruit. The sounder the grapes are the less sulphite is required. It is quite easy to determine how much sugar to add by pressing some of the grapes and testing the gravity of the juice. The pulp and the syrup are transferred to an open vat or barrel with the head removed, the sulphite is added and this is followed by a yeast culture. The most important task now is to prevent undue access of air to the skins which will float up. As mentioned earlier, a perforated disc of wood called a sinker can be used to hold this cap down or a lattice-work of wood, which fits into the top of the barrel, will effect a similar result. Failing that the cap must be pushed down two or three times a day so as to enable colour to be extracted and prevent vinegar formation in the cap which is exposed to air. A large funnel placed downwards at the bottom of the container can also be used to prevent the cap from remaining dry and assist in keeping it soaked with the fermenting juice. The stem of the funnel should protrude a little above the cap or a short piece of rubber tube can be attached to make it do so. As the yeast, which will ferment from the base of the liquid, produces gas this will push some of the fermenting wine through the stem of the funnel and thus keep the cap covered with liquid. The fermentation will take anything from five days to a fortnight and it is advisable to draw the wine off and press the pulp while there is still some sugar in the liquid. A gravity between 5 and 10 degrees is a suitable one for drawing off. The reason for this is that the red colour of a wine is quickly affected by air and will turn insoluble and brown. To preserve a good colour therefore it is desirable to prevent any access of air and during active fermentation there is still enough gas coming off to protect the wine. If it is desired to have a mild wine the pulp must not be pressed too much as a good bit of the tannin will then remain behind in the pulp. On the other hand the later pressings can be used to add to a milder wine or be matured separately and used for balancing any red wine lacking in tannin. The more tannin the wine contains, and there is a good bit present in the pips and in the skins, the longer will it take to mature but the better will be the eventual flavour. French wine producers generally add some white of egg as soon as the wine is drawn off into barrels, usually the whisked-up white of one egg to about 10 gallons of wine. The containers should then be left bung full and the fermentation will complete during the warm autumn and during the cold weather the wine will clear. The first racking should be as soon as incipient clarification has taken place as the longer the wine remains on the yeast deposit the more will it tend to lose colour. Therefore in red wine production it is highly undesirable to stir up the yeast deposit prior to racking. If the wine is too sour a little of the acid can be removed by the addition of about a quarter ounce of chalk to a gallon of wine, or this chalk can be added to the juice prior to fermentation.

For red wine fermentation it is highly desirable to use a sedimentary wine yeast and the finest red wines are made by using a Pommard yeast. This is a yeast which ferments very slowly and is particularly sedimentary and will not float up into the liquid either during the fermentation in casks or at racking time. It must be emphasized that during red wine production fermentation sometimes sticks; invariably this is due to too much heat being formed during the vigorous fermentation. In large scale production cooling coils have to be used and no producer of red wine would let his wine ferment without testing its temperature twice daily. Once a wine has stuck it is very difficult to get it to ferment again and it is then preferable to draw off and press the pulp and start the juice fermenting in the following manner. First of all, a new yeast culture must be prepared and some of the juice which has been drawn off can be used for the liquid to be added to the culture. It is brought to the boil to remove all alcohol and a nutrient added and this solution added to a bottle culture. Once this is fermenting well the actively fermenting wine is transferred to a gallon jar and a couple of pints of the stuck wine is added to it. When this is properly fermenting the jar can then be nearly filled and when this in turn is in active fermentation it can be added to, say, 9 gallons of the stuck wine. It is only by adding the wine in stages that one can ensure active fermentation. The amateur will, of course, not have any equipment to enable him to cool his juice such as is used in commercial production. This generally consists of coils which are either inside the fermenting vats where cold water runs through them or the wine can be drawn off through coils immersed in cold brine and be returned after cooling to the bulk of the fermentation. In amateur wine production a plastic pail or bowl filled with cold water, or in extreme cases with a little ice water, will soon reduce the temperature below the danger point. In no case should it exceed 86° Fahrenheit (30° Centigrade) for more than a very short period. Cooling is generally begun at 85–90° Fahrenheit

(29–32° C.) and the wine is cooled to between 75 and 80° F. (24–27° C.).

Just as white wines need to be tested for stability so also should red wines be examined in the same way, particularly to see that no colour change occurs. If there is any sign of browning then at least 1 Campden tablet should be added to a gallon of wine prior to racking and if necessary this may have to be repeated at the second racking, but provided the fruit has been sound and free from mould there will be very little tendency to browning in a wine which is being made according to the foregoing directions. All wines made from grapes must be chilled prior to bottling so as to remove the cream of tartar. Grapes used for red wine production should be the small-berried wine grapes but if greenhouse dessert grapes are used the wines will only be pink as the proportion of skin to juice in dessert grapes is very much less than in wine grapes. This difficulty can be quite easily overcome by pressing out half the juice from dessert grapes and fermenting it for a white wine and using the pulp with the remainder of the juice for red wine production.

THE PRODUCTION OF SWEET DESSERT WINE FROM GRAPES

Sauterne types of wine must be made from really ripe grapes and particularly from grapes which have gone mouldy in a suitable manner. As mentioned earlier the juice of ripe grapes which have been attacked by *Bortrytis cinerea* will become very much sweeter and also very much less acid. Outdoor grapes in this country will not ripen sufficiently to undergo such an 'ennobling process' but anyone with a greenhouse can make his grapes go mouldy *after ripening* by inducing moist and hot conditions in the greenhouse by closing down during sunny periods. Such grapes cannot be removed from the stalks and have to be pressed whole and the juice will ferment rather more slowly than normally, but will clarify quite quickly. At least three Campden tablets must be added to each gallon of juice. Another method of obtaining a Sauterne-like character is to let the grapes dry out by laying them on straw or paper in a hot, dry shed or room. During such storage the juice will become more concentrated and less sour. For Sauterne-type wines it is as well not to add a yeast nutrient but a sedimentary wine yeast culture is again needed. The gravity should be brought up by the addition of concentrated syrup to 135 or more, but not above 150. If the fermentation is very rapid then chilling may slow it down and may help the yeast to settle. Once the yeast has partly settled it is possible to draw the wine off the deposit and thus slow the fermentation down. This interrupted fermentation can be carried out when the gravity is round about 60 but the earlier it is done the greater is the danger of the wine not fermenting to a suitable alcohol content. Sweet wines will tend to be rather unstable unless the alcohol content is around 15 per cent by volume or just over 12 per cent by weight, so the amateur wine maker who has tested the gravity of his wine at the start will know that this alcohol concentration is reached when the gravity has dropped by about 110 points (see page 87). If therefore the original gravity of the juice was 150 then the wine will be stable at a gravity of about 15. This gravity will not be reached in the first few weeks and in fact it may take six months and require the return of warm weather before the wine will finally ferment out; but with the method of racking and storage which has been described and with intermediate testing for stability to air even quite sweet wines will become stable. Such sweet wines should not be bottled before they are a year old and they also must undergo a period of chilling so as to throw out the cream of tartar. The Sauternes of commerce are kept in barrels for about 3 years and racked three or four times a year because wine which lies on its lees too long, unless fortified, may develop a foul taste due to the yeast dissolving. (Note that Sherries on the other hand are not racked from their yeast deposit but are normally fortified to 17 per cent of alcohol prior to maturing and this prevents the development of off flavours due to the decomposition of yeast.)

THE PRODUCTION OF SPARKLING WINE

As mentioned earlier, sparkling wines such as Champagne are made by a process of double fermentation. The wine is nearly always made from the juice of red grapes as the small amount of red pigment which will get into the juice confers a characteristic flavour on the wine. It can just as well be made from the juice of white grapes but the flavour will be slightly different. The juice if fermented with a champagne yeast starter and the requisite amount of syrup to give a wine with about 9–10 per cent of alcohol. A small amount of sulphite should be added and a teaspoonful of yeast nutrient per gallon. The wine will go dry and throw its deposit of yeast and cream of tartar during the cold weather and become practically clear. The wine is now racked into a fresh container and if it is desired to make the sparkling wine in a barrel then the requisite amount of sugar is added. A fresh yeast culture is not necessary as a new yeast crop will usually form, but should it not do so then a new one is required. It is obvious, of course, that the wine in barrel will tend to lose its gas on opening, hence most champagne is made in bottles or in small half or one gallon containers so that the contents can be consumed immediately on opening. For the amateur wine maker strong cider flagons can be used and the wine, to which the sugar and yeast have been added and which has stood in a warm place for a few days to encourage the start of fresh fermentation, is then drawn off into these flagons and allowed to ferment for a considerable period. There should be about an inch of head space over the liquid and if the flagon is closed down with a well-fitting screw stopper then the bottle can be stood upright. If on the other hand corks are used then these have to be wired down; nowadays hollow-centred plastic corks are most suitable and the bottles can be stood upright if it is not intended to remove the yeast. If it is to be removed eventually, standing them upside down will facilitate this. The best temperature for the production of sparkling wine is below 60° F. as not only is there less likely to be breakage of bottles but also the wine will hold its gas better on pouring out. The slower the fermentation the better will be the quality. For champagnization allow between 2 and 3½ oz. of sugar to each gallon of wine but it is safer to use the smaller quantity. About a saltspoonful of isinglass added to each gallon of wine sometimes helps to hold the yeast deposit down. Amateurs will generally not wish to remove the yeast as this is a long and wearisome process and requires skill. It is done by shaking down the yeast till it becomes a firm deposit on or in the cork and that can only be done by giving the bottles twists over a period of time and gradually removing them from the horizontal to the vertical with the corks pointing downwards. By putting the neck of the bottle into a freezing mixture it is possible to freeze the yeast deposit on to the cork and by cutting the wires the cork will fly out and has at once to be replaced by another cork which is wired in place. It is usual to fill up the bottle with a little sweetened alcohol to replace that lost and also to provide a slight sweetness as the champagne will be otherwise quite dry. It is of course not possible to carry out this method of freezing when screw stoppers are used but if the bottles are kept upright the yeast deposit should remain fairly firmly adherent to the base, when most of the champagne can be poured off clear. Champagne should always be chilled before pouring as that helps to retain the gas and makes the wine more attractive to drink.

THE PRODUCTION OF FORTIFIED WINES, SHERRY AND PORT

Fortified wines are wines to which alcohol has been added. They can be broadly classed into Port type wines and Sherry type wines.

Sherry

Sherries may range from light coloured wines such as a Fino, which has undergone a period of maturing under a yeast film, to dark and sweet wines such as an Oloroso. The latter are often marketed under the name of Cream sherries. To make sherry it is desirable for the grapes to be as ripe as possible and if it is not convenient to dry the grapes then a method which can be used by amateurs is to mince some raisins and soak them in some fresh grape juice for a few days and press out the juice. As the amount of sugar extracted in soaking and pressing will vary, no exact figures can be given as to the quantity of raisins required but half a pound added to a gallon of juice should suffice. The juice is next tested for its gravity and brought up to a gravity of 116. It may be necessary to add a little acid if this is lacking, particularly if some raisins have been used as they are low in acid. From half to one teaspoonful of yeast energizer should then be added and a sherry yeast culture is required to obtain a good sherry flavour. The fermentation is likely to proceed quickly and will go nearly to dryness. The wine is then allowed to clarify after which it is drawn off its yeast deposit and transferred to another container. When making sherry no sulphite should be used unless the grapes have been mouldy and then not more than one tablet per gallon. The difference between obtaining sherry flavours and white wine flavours is that in white wine production the greatest care is taken to prevent access of air, while sherry fermentation is carried out in the presence of air both by having the container only three-quarters full and also instead of using a fermentation trap filled with water an empty fermentation trap is employed, but the neck of the top is lightly plugged with cotton wool to prevent access of vinegar flies. When the wine has been drawn off its first yeast deposit it is transferred to another container which should not be full and which is stood in a warm place. New yeast will grow and under certain conditions this yeast will start to float to the top and may form a wrinkled skin. Unlike the skin from flowers of wine the film-forming sherry yeast will produce a cream-coloured skin which may later turn brown, but sometimes only small islands of yeasts float on the surface but are sufficient to give a fino character to the sherry. In that case the sherry will become pale in colour and develop particularly fine flavours. A still better method of en-couraging skin formation is to add some grape concentrate instead of sugar to the new wine. Grape concentrate contains generally about 60 per cent sugar so betweeen 3½ per cent and 4 per cent added to the wine will give sufficient sugar to encourage yeast growth.

An Oloroso sherry is one which has matured in air but has not grown a film. Such sherries darken with age and can be rendered sweet by the addition of grape concentrate or some sugar. The amateur can make his own grape concentrate by boiling up raisins or currants with a minimum amount of water, pressing out the juice and, if necessary, letting the juice simmer until it becomes thick and syrupy.

Sherries made as above should contain about 15 per cent of alcohol but by starting with a gravity of 130 instead of 120 the alcohol percentage may go up to about 17 per cent prior to the addition of extra sugar or grape concentrate, which may lead to a slightly higher percentage still. But it is usual to fortify sherries during the time that they are maturing by bringing the alcohol up to between 18 per cent and 20 per cent. Fortification is of course not cheap. It is best to use a neutral spirit such as Vodka 80 proof or Polish Spirit 100 or 140 proof for fortification as these spirits lack any overriding flavour.

FORTIFICATION AND ITS COST—THE USE OF THE PEARSON SQUARE

Fortification, whether carried out to a certain alcohol strength by volume or to a certain degree of proof spirit, is quite simple to calculate by the use of the Pearson Square, but care must always be taken to use corresponding figures and not to get them mixed. Wine can either be fortified to, say, 18 per cent of alcohol by volume when the alcohol by volume of the fortifying spirit must be known, or the fortification can be carried out to a certain degree of proof spirit when the strength of the alcohol used must also be calculated in terms of proof spirit.

As an example place at the top left hand corner (A) of the

square the strength of the fortifying alcohol, say 90 per cent. In the corner below (B) place the strength of the wine to be fortified, say 15 per cent, and in the centre at (C) the final strength required, perhaps 19 per cent. By subtracting (B) from (C) the quantity of alcohol needed is placed at (D) in the top right hand corner i.e. $19-15=4=(D)$. By subtracting (C) from (A) $90-19=71=$ (E), the quantity of wine to be used for fortifying is obtained. In other words, to 71 gallons or ounces of the wine 4 gallons or ounces of the strong alcohol have to be added to give a wine of 19 per cent alcohol content. This would be about right for sherries but ports sometimes contain up to 22 per cent of alcohol by volume.

PEARSON SQUARE

(A) 90%	4(D)
(C) 19%	
(B) 15%	71 (E)

It does not make much difference to the cost whether pure alcohol, Polish Spirit or Vodka is used for the fortification. Ninety per cent alcohol is 157·8 proof but as it is easier to buy Polish Spirit from a wine merchant at 140 proof, or 80 per cent alcohol by volume, the use of the latter is advocated.

Taking a different example and using the Pearson Square again, a wine of 18 per cent alcohol by volume fortified to 20 per cent using 90 per cent spirit requires 2 parts of spirit to 70 parts of wine or a gallon of wine will need to have $4\frac{1}{2}$ oz. of 90 per cent spirit added to it. This $4\frac{1}{2}$ oz. will cost 12s. 4d. and as a gallon is suffi-cient to fill 6 wine bottles, the cost per bottle is 2s. 1d. On the other hand if the wine had only contained 15 per cent of alcohol the cost of fortification to 20 per cent would be $2\frac{1}{2}$ times as much. This emphasizes the importance of attaining as high alcohol content as possible prior to fortification.

TABLE XI

THE ALCOHOL CONTENT OF WINES AND SPIRITS AND
CORRESPONDING DEGREES OF PROOF SPIRIT

Percentage Proof Spirit	Percentage Alcohol by Volume	Percentage Alcohol by Weight
157·8	90·0	85·7
140·2	80·0	73·5
122·7	70·0	62·4
113·9	65	57·2
105·1	60	52·1
96·3	55	47·2
87·6	50	42·5
78·8	45	37·9
70·0	40	33·4
61·2	35	29·0
52·4	30	24·7
43·8	25	20·5
35·0	20	16·3
33·1	19	15·4
31·4	18	14·6
29·7	17	13·8
28·0	16	13·0
26·2	15	12·1
24·5	14	11·3
22·7	13	10·5
21·6	12	9·7
19·3	11	8·9
17·4	10	8·0
15·7	9	7·2
13·9	8	6·4
12·3	7	5·6
10·5	6	4·8
8·8	5	4·0
7·0	4	3·2
5·2	3	2·4
3·5	2	1·6
1·74	1	0·8

As a rough approximation, within the range of alcohol concentrations which occur in wines, the percentage of alcohol by weight can be converted into percentage of alcohol by volume by multiplying by 1·25. In the higher alcohol ranges this does not apply because when alcohol and water are mixed there is a shrinkage in volume and heat is liberated.

Also alcohol by volume can be converted into proof spirit by multiplying by 1·75.

Thus a solution containing 15·5 per cent of alcohol by volume is equivalent to 27·1 per cent proof spirit (15·5 × 1·75 = 27·1).

Obviously the reverse also holds good, the percentage of alcohol by volume corresponding to a known percentage of proof spirit is found by dividing by 1·75.

Port wines

Are made by a slightly different method of fortification. Originally port wine was introduced into this country by a shipper who liked the sweet red dessert wines of Portugal and to ensure that they were stable during shipment some grape spirit or brandy was added. It was found that these wines improved not only in stability but that on maturing particularly good flavours developed and hence port wines were made by a system of fortification, but instead of adding the spirit to the finished wine it is now added during the early stages of fermentation. The sweet grape juice is fermented in the presence of the skins but long before the sugar has gone alcohol is added to stop the fermentation. This means that the wine will not only remain sweet but will retain some of its rich mucilagenous nature and fermentation will be arrested, anyhow for a while. When it restarts another lot of alcohol is added. It is not possible for an amateur to make a port by these methods mainly because fortification is much too expensive, secondly because English grapes are too sour and too much lacking in sugar, and thirdly because much analytical control is required. On the other hand, if red grape wine is made by the normal methods and a further amount of red grape pulp is brought to the boil in a saucepan so as to extract the red colour and then treated with, say, half an ounce of chalk to the gallon to remove the acid this juice can be filtered, sweetened with about a pound of sugar to two pints and then added to the red wine. There will be some renewed fermentation but the juice which has been added will make the wine somewhat richer in body. When the wine has fermented out then some alcohol can be added to bring the concentration up to between 18 per cent and 20 per cent.

Wine from Grape Prunings

The author has made a very attractive white wine which was not unlike a hock from the prunings of greenhouse grapes cut off when they were about the size of peas. 3 lb. of these prunings occupied 48 oz. in volume. They were boiled with 48 oz. of water and the pulp pressed when cold. Two and a half pints of juice resulted and, as the acid was about 1¾ per cent, 3 pints of water, 2½ lb. of sugar and 1 teaspoonful of yeast nutrient were added. This resulted in a juice of a gravity of 100. It was fermented with a sedimentary wine yeast and on completion a Campden tablet was added to the wine.

Grape Foliage Wine

Some purists do not consider wine made from anything but ripe grapes as wine, but the author has tasted a most delicious light hock made from the leaves and tendrils of an outdoor vine, the directions given to me being:

To make approximately one gallon.

Pour 8 pints of boiling water over 5 lb. of leaves and tendrils, leave for 24 hours, press and wash the cake with another pint of warm water. Dissolve in this 3½ lb. of sugar. The gravity should be about 100. Add a Campden tablet, ½ teaspoonful of yeast nutrient, a wine yeast and leave in a warm place for 2 days, then remove to a cooler place to ferment slowly using, of course, a fermentation trap and seeing that the containers are full. When it has clarified, rack, bung down and rack again prior to bottling. To ensure a sound fermentation it might be wise to add 1 lb. of raisins to the leaves because the latter are a little lacking in the natural yeast foods.

The Production of Vermouth

Dry wines, especially if they have gone a little dark and oxidized and have thus lost much of their fine fresh flavour, can be used to make vermouth. Herbs containing vermouth are obtainable and very little is needed to give a flavour to the wine. As little as 1 per cent of the herbs are soaked in the wine which is then sweetened according to taste with strong syrup. It is better to soak the herbs in the wine for a day or two rather than in water as the higher the alcohol concentration is, the more stable will the wine be. It may be of interest to know the ingredients of a vermouth powder and many a wine maker will like to mix his own herbs. Five ounces of vermouth (or wormwood) are mixed with 1 ounce of dried and powdered balm leaf, 1 ounce of powdered gentian, a quarter ounce of dried yarrow blossom, dried angelica root, dried camomile and dried tonka beans. Traces of cloves, nutmeg, cinnamon and thyme may also be added while some vermouth powders also contain spearmint or peppermint in very small proportions. The herbs can be put into a bag and soaked for a few hours with barely enough warer to cover them, and then hung for a few days in the wine. An ounce and a half to 2 ounces of herbs to a gallon of wine are suitable. The sugar content of vermouth ranges between 4 per cent and 18 per cent and generally it is fortified to round about 18–22 per cent of alcohol by volume, that is 31·4–38·5 per cent proof spirit.

FRUIT WINES OF VARIOUS TYPES

It is desirable, when making wine from various fruits to take some cognisance of the fact that some fruits lend themselves better to one type of wine than others. For instance, if it is desired to make a port type of wine, richly coloured red fruit like damsons, bilberries or elderberries are more suitable than, for instance, strawberries or light-coloured cherries. Fruits which have a very penetrating flavour, such as raspberries, should be used for a sweet wine and, as far as possible, the characteristic flavour of the fruit should be retained. Fruits which are very lacking in flavour, like white currants and pears, lend themselves better to a white table wine than would, for instance, the juice of a crab apple or a strongly flavoured dessert apple. On the other hand, one can make use of apples for table wine production by reducing the flavour by the addition of syrup or choosing a cooking apple with very little characteristic flavour. Fruit wine making is more difficult because one can overdo the addition of syrup by not having tested the juice for its sugar concentration, but provided a little care is taken every bit as good wines can be made from English fruits as are made from grapes.

Anyone interested in wine making will decide the type of wine they like and choose fruit accordingly. For instance, for dry red wines bilberries are used very extensively on the Continent and these also make a very attractive sweet wine similar to a port. Another fruit which is suitable for red wine is red currants provided some blackcurrants or some elderberry juice is added as otherwise the wine would be quite pale. It is possible to make a wine from red currants which looks and tastes like a claret and after sufficient maturing even experts cannot detect that the wine has not been made from grapes. Apples will make a very nice dessert wine or can be used for producing sweet and dry sherries. Rhubarb is particularly good for dessert wines of the sauterne type or for sparkling wines similar to champagne. From green gooseberries one can make dry table wine or champagne, while apples are also used for sparkling wines. Plums lend themselves very well to dessert wines and so do blackberries, loganberries and raspberries. Strawberries and ripe gooseberries both tend to give a wine of sherrylike quality. Orange wine is produced from the juice of oranges to which some syrup and perhaps extra acid has to be added; the peel should not be added to the wine until it has finished fermenting as the orange oil sometimes stops fermentation. Raisins, dates and figs can all be used for wine making but acid has to be added and the minced fruit must be thoroughly soaked in boiling water to extract all the sugar from it. Full details of the various wines, arranged in alphabetical order, are given in the following, but it must be remembered that the same recipe can give different results as the sugar content of fruits can vary considerably and the sugar-juice mixture should be tested by the wine maker prior to fermentation. Provided the sugar addition is right, a pure wine yeast is used and both acid and yeast nutrient are added where necessary, the production of both sweet and dry wines should present no difficulties. Formulae for the production of fruit wines are given in Tables V and VI, but more details on handling the fruit and adjusting the juice will be found in the following recipes. Some wines which have too high an initial gravity are included as these will assist the wine maker to appreciate how this affects the fermentation and will show the steps necessary to remedy the fault.

Apple Wine

If it is desired to make a dry wine from apples the juice should be pressed out of the minced apple and tested for gravity. Two Campden tablets should be added to the pulp, then sufficient syrup to bring the gravity up to between 80 and 90, a sedimentary wine yeast and yeast nutrient are added and the wine is fermented to a gravity of about 10 and then racked into a fresh cask or container. Some wine makers prefer to let the wine stay on its yeast until it is quite dry and rack off in the spring. Just as in grape wines it is desirable to test the wine for its stability to air; if it darkens on exposure in an open glass then a Campden tablet should be added. Even if the wine appears dry there is very likely to be a certain amount of sugar and even a dry wine must be racked at least a second time before bottling. For a sweet apple wine additional syrup can be added to the dry wine to bring the gravity up again by another 30–40. If the original gravity of the wine was 100 then by bringing it up by, say 40, is equivalent to an original gravity of 140. There is no reason why the wine should not be fermented to dryness first and then some syrup added, in fact this method of subsequent addition of syrup is conducive to producing wines of high alcohol content and good flavour. The wine can also be rendered sparkling in a manner similar to that used in the case of grape wine by adding 1¼ oz. of strong syrup to each pint of wine, that is, 10 oz. to a gallon. The same methods of bottling in strong bottles must, of course, be employed. Other fruit can be added to apple such as black-berries, loganberries, raspberries or plums to make wines of different character and colour.

A practical example of making a sweet apple wine may prove of interest. The apples were minced and the juice had a gravity of 66. This dropped down to nil in seven days. Syrup was then added to increase the gravity considerably so as to obtain a sweet wine. This can be achieved by using 2 parts of juice and 1 part of a strong syrup of a gravity of 300. The effective gravity of the syrup would be one-third of 300 = 100 and of the juice would be two-thirds of 66 = 44. Therefore the wine will be sweet having been made from a juice which is equivalent to one having an original gravity of 144.

Apricot Wine

Apricots are rich in pectin so Pectozyme is required. 2 lb. of dried or 4 lb. of fresh apricots are brought to the boil with 4 pints of water till thoroughly soft. The brew is cooled to 30° C., 1 table-spoonful of Pectozyme, ½lb. sugar, an all purpose yeast and yeast energizer are added. It is then left in a warm airing cupboard for four days with stirring and strained off. 2½ pints of syrup are next added and the brew made up to 1 gallon.

Another recipe uses only 2 lb. of dried apricots or 4 lb. of fresh apricots with 4 pints of boiling water and 1 lb. of sugar. Pectozyme is added and a sherry yeast is used and the fermentation carried out in the presence of the pulp for a week. The mixture is strained and made up to a gallon, a teaspoonful of yeast energizer and 2½ pints of strong syrup are added and the brew is fermented to completion. (The strong syrup is made from 4 lb. of sugar added to 2 pints of water.)

Wine makers who do not like the strong flavour of apricot can mix about 2 lb. of apricots with 2 lb. of raisins and ferment this mixture.

Bilberry Wine (Dry) Claret type

Bilberries make a very fine dry red wine and 3 lb. of fruit should be allowed for 1 gallon of wine.

The bilberries should be washed, brought to the boil with 2 pints of water and 1 lb. of sugar. One teaspoonful of yeast energizer and one Campden tablet are added and the brew fermented with a sedimentary wine yeast for one week after which it is pressed. The yield should be about four pints. An equal quantity of syrup of gravity 100 should next be added and the fermentation allowed to continue to dryness. When completed in about fourteen days the wine should be racked. After a further two months the wine will have deposited a second crop of yeast and so it must be racked again. Already the bilberry flavour will have been replaced by a claret flavour but the wine will improve considerably with a third racking, after which a Campden tablet should be added prior to bottling.

Bilberry Wine (Sweet) Port type

The hardest part about making bilberry wine is the picking of the berries. To reduce this herculean task a little, a sweet bilberry wine was made with a somewhat smaller quantity of berries, i.e. 5 lb. to make 2 gallons. This wine, being sweet, requires a little added acid and ½ oz. of citric acid should be added to the 2 gallon brew.

To 5 lb. of bilberries allow 3¼ pints of water, 1¼ lb. of sugar, 1 pint of syrup (gravity 300) and ½ oz. of citric acid. Bring to the boil, cool, add 2 teaspoonsful of yeast energizer and a port wine yeast and allow the mixture to ferment for a week. Press through a coarse linen bag. The yield was 8 pints 8 oz. Add 4¾ pints of syrup of gravity 300 and 3 pints of water when the fermentation should continue slowly. On completion of the fermentation a wine of port-like character should be obtained.

Bilberry Wine, *semi-sweet*

As has been stressed repeatedly the wine maker should test his recipe as the fruit juice used may, especially in dry hot years, be richer in sugar with consequent higher gravity than in cold wet years. In one case the amount of sugar advocated in a particular recipe produced a juice with a gravity of 195. This was much too high and although fermentation started it stopped after the gravity had dropped only 10 degrees as the yeast cannot deal with such a heavy sugar concentration.

Date	Gravity	
Aug. 23rd	195	
Aug. 28th	185	Fermentation stopped.
		Added 2 pints of water which reduced the gravity to 113 and allowed fermentation to proceed.
Aug. 28th	113	
Sept. 1st	90	
Sept. 16th	72	
Sept. 30th	61	
Nov. 23rd	24	Racked.
Jan. 23rd	15	Racked again, added 1 Campden tablet and bottled.

The result was a moderately sweet and full bodied dark red wine of quite surprisingly fine flavour.

Blackberry Wine

Blackberries should be used either for a sweet dessert wine, in which case a sedimentary wine yeast is advised, or for a dry or sweet sherry type of wine for which a sherry yeast is necessary. This fruit contains a good bit of tannin so it is not desirable to ferment more than 48 hours on the pulp. To 6 lb. of blackberries 4 lb. of sugar can be added and a gallon of water for the making of a sweet wine. The following gravity figures show the progress of a wine made to this formula and using a wine yeast.

Date	Gravity	
July 18th	165	
July 22nd	118	
July 26th	115	
Aug. 3rd	110	
Aug. 23rd	91	
Sept. 1st	88	
Sept. 16th	86	Because this wine was started at a rather high gravity, fermentation had become sluggish, so 1 pint of water was added which helped it to proceed.
Sept. 16th	81	
Sept. 30th	76	
Nov. 23rd	45	Still fermenting. Racked.
May 12th	28	Still fermenting very slightly but excellent flavour.

The wine was just clearing and was ready for the second racking in a month's time. It was first racked at a gravity of 45 so as to slow down the fermentation and develop wine-like flavours.

Blackberry Sherry

It was decided to make a dry blackberry wine according to the following formula:

3lb. blackberries were brought to the boil with 2 pints water and ½ lb. sugar. This made approximately 4 pints. A teaspoonful of yeast nutrient was added and a sherry yeast, the fermentation being allowed to proceed for a couple of days. On pressing the juice had a gravity of 79 which in a fortnight went down to below 1. The product was rather bitter and it was decided to dilute by adding more syrup, 1½ pints of strong syrup being used; this brought the gravity up to 82.

Date	Gravity
Sept. 16th	82
Sept. 30th	50
Nov. 23rd	·987 (i.e. below 1).

The wine was quite dry and clear and was racked from its yeast deposit. It tasted very sherry-like and it was decided to bottle it after a second racking. Some maturing will ensure a still greater improvement in flavour.

Some wine makers like to add spices to their wine and the following recipe may prove of interest.

Blackberry Wine (Spiced)

To 4 lb. of blackberries add ½ gallon of strong syrup and ½ gallon of water, ½ oz. of root ginger, the juice of two lemons, 4 to 5 cloves and some cinnamon. Bring all this to the boil and strain. Add a wine yeast, preferably also a teaspoonful of yeast nutrient and ferment to completion.

Cherry Wine

Cherries make a particularly attractive wine and if sweet cherries are used it is best to use the dark ones, while for a light-coloured wine sour cherries are preferable. When using the dark cherries either some citric acid or lemon juice or some sour cherries must be added, as otherwise the wine will not ferment in a satisfactory manner. The cherries are pulped and about 10 per cent of the stones may be broken and added to the pulp. This is followed by one or two Campden tablets and a wine yeast and fermentation is carried out in the presence of the pulp for from 2–4 days. Cherry wines can be either sweet or dry and here again the addition of strong syrup facilitates the production of a suitable formula. One can reckon that the gravity of the cherry juice is about 50, unless the cherries are very sweet when it may be as much as 70, and that for a dry wine the gravity should be increased to about 100 while for a sweet wine the equivalent of an original gravity of from 140–160 is desirable. It is best not to use a sherry yeast nor to ferment in air but rather to ferment the wine under a water seal and use a wine yeast so as to retain the characteristic cherry flavour. To make one gallon of dry cherry wine with a cherry juice of gravity 50 allow 6½ pints of juice and 1½ pints of strong syrup. This will bring the gravity to 97 according to the following calculation.

$$\begin{array}{r} 6\frac{1}{2} \times \ 50 = 325 \\ \underline{1\frac{1}{2} \times 300 = 450} \\ 8 \qquad 775 \end{array}$$

Divide by
$$8 = \ 97$$

For a sweet wine the corresponding proportions would be 5 pints of cherry juice of gravity 50 to 3 pints of strong syrup.

$$\begin{array}{r} 5 \times \ 50 = 250 \\ \underline{3 \times 300 = 900} \\ 8 \qquad 1150 \end{array}$$

Divide by
$$8 = 144$$

CURRANT WINES, BLACK, WHITE AND RED

Blackcurrant Wine

2 lb. of fruit were mixed with 2 pints of water, 1 pint strong syrup, and 1 teaspoonful yeast nutrient. The juice was drawn by boiling, a sedimentary wine yeast was added after cooling and the fermentation was carried out on the skins for four days. After pressing two pints of strong syrup were added and gravity readings were obtained as follows

Date	Gravity	
July 6th	118	
July 16th	105	
Sept. 19th	21	1 Campden tablet was added.
Dec. 5th	9	

The wine was clear but not brilliant, so was filtered through pulp and bottled.

Another useful recipe for Blackcurrant Wine is as follows:

To 2½ lb. blackcurrants add 1¾ pints water and ½ lb. sugar. Draw the juice by boiling and when cool add a teaspoonful of yeast nutrient. Here again a sedimentary wine yeast is necessary so as to obtain a wine with a good strong colour. Fermentation is carried out on the skins for three days when the mixture is pressed and should result in 3 pints of juice. 3 pints of strong syrup were added and fermentation continued slowly but quite steadily, but as the starting gravity was higher than it should have been fermentation ceased after a while although there was much unfermented sugar present. This necessitated the addition of some water to enable the yeast to continue the fermentation. The following fermentation records may prove of interest and will again show how the wine maker can control results. Undoubtedly it would have been better if more water had been added in the first instance and instead of adding 3 pints syrup, a pint of syrup and a pint of water would have been a better proportion. Although a gravity of up to 160 is recommended for sweet wines it must be remembered that some of the sugar already present would have been converted to alcohol during the fermentation on the pulp so in the above recipe the total original gravity would be well above 160.

Date	Gravity
July 18th	165
July 22nd	118
July 26th	115
Aug. 3rd	110
Aug. 23rd	91
Sept. 1st	91
Sept. 16th	91

One pint of water was then added as quite evidently the yeast could not deal with the sugar present. This encouraged renewed fermentation as follows:

Date	Gravity	
Sept. 16th	81	due to addition of water.
Sept. 30th	76	
Nov. 23rd	45	
June 12th	28	Still fermenting slightly.

This clarified as a sweet wine and was bottled in the autumn.[1]

Red Currant Wine. Dry (Claret type)

To make 4½ gallons of red currant wine allow 8 lb. red currants, 4 lb. blackcurrants, 2½ gallons water, 10 lb. sugar and ½ oz. yeast nutrient. Boil the above ingredients together and when cool add a sedimentary wine yeast. Ferment for a week and press. The fermentation proceeded as follows:

Date	Gravity
June 6th	110
June 16th	95
Sept. 8th	Below .

The wine was racked and two Campden tablets added. The gravity dropped to 0·998 by the 5th December. The wine was racked again and bottled in April.

White Currant Wine

4 lb. of white currants were stripped, the fruit pulped and pressed. The pulp was mixed with a pint of water and re-pressed. The total yield was 40 oz., i.e. 2 pints, and the gravity was 36. The juice was extremely sour, containing about 2¼ per cent of acid. It was therefore mixed with 5 pints of water and 3 lb. of sugar. The gravity was then 110. A teaspoonful of yeast nutrient was added and a sedimentary wine yeast culture. This fermented to a good and practically dry white wine.

---

[1] The examples of wines with high gravity are given to show that high gravities produce sticking and this can be overcome by the addition of water. Normally an initial gravity of 140 is high enough for a sweet wine.

White Currant Wine (Skins only)

As it was considered that a good wine could be made from a second pressing of the white currant pulp another pint of water was added and the pulp re-pressed. This yielded 1 pint to which were added 3 pints of water, 2 lb. of sugar, 2 teaspoonfuls of yeast nutrient and a wine yeast. The gravity was 125 and fermentation proceeded as follows:

Date	Gravity	
July 9th	125	
		During this period yeast was growing.
July 11th	125	
July 16th	114	
Sept 19th	60	The wine showed slight darkening so one Campden tablet was added.
Dec. 5th	44	Fermentation sluggish because wine contained too much pectin.
Mar. 3rd	32	

The flavour was very good but the wine had not cleared well nor did filtration with asbestos pulp give a good result and this was undoubtedly due to the presence of pectin. This can be removed by the addition of a heaped tablespoonful of Pectozyme to the wine which is kept in a warm airing cupboard for a few days. By subsequent fining with Serena Wine Finings the wine can be rendered clear and quite brilliant.

Damson Wine

A wine which is a particular favourite in fruit growing districts is damson wine in its various forms. Both dry and sweet damson wines are attractive provided the fermentation is carried out with a suitable yeast and the duration of the fermentation on the pulp is kept short. Two days' active fermentation will suffice but the wine maker will have to use his judgment. Sufficient colour should be extracted during the pulp fermentation to give a brightly coloured wine but the brew should not taste bitter. Damsons are rather acid and some of this can be removed by the addition of chalk, preferably after pressing the pulp. Half an ounce of chalk added to a gallon of the juice will settle with the yeast deposit and can be racked off. For a dry wine allow a total of about three pounds of sugar to the gallon and for a sweet wine from four to five pounds of sugar will suffice.

For a dry wine a Pommard wine yeast is indicated while for a sweet wine a Port or Malaga or Madeira yeast is suitable.

Damson Wine, Dry

4 lb. of damsons, 1 gallon boiling water, 1 teaspoonful of yeast nutrient, 1 lb. of sugar. Simply bruise the fruit, pour the boiling water over them, add the other ingredients and when cool add a wine yeast. Ferment for two days and press. To each gallon of juice allow 2½ lb. of sugar. The gravity should be well below 100, preferably about 80 to 85 as some of the sugar which was present during the pulp fermentation will have already been converted into alcohol.

For a *sweet damson wine* the same directions hold good but the sugar is increased to four or five pounds.

Date Wine

Dates ferment very well but, of course, they contain a good deal of sugar and have to be boiled with water to extract this and to reduce the sugar content to a suitable level. Also, the wine will be rather expensive unless some of the dates are replaced by cane sugar and furthermore as dates are lacking in acid this also has to be added; about one ounce of citric acid to each gallon of brew would be about correct. The dates are brought to the boil with water allowing from two to three pints to each pound of dates and adding half a pound of cane sugar. Dates make a good sherry type of wine and a sherry yeast should therefore be employed.

Elderberry Wine

Elderberries ferment quite well and have, of course, a good colour, but they are often rather bitter. Sometimes when the wine has been adjusted to make a dry wine it may prove very unpalatable. In that case it can be fermented on with the addition of some more syrup and a wine will be produced which is much milder and still of good colour. By adding sufficient syrup it may even be possible to make a wine which is not unlike a port. The following gives the gravities obtained when treating a dry elderberry wine with further syrup and which resulted in a wine with a distinctly port-like flavour. Originally 4 lb. of elderberries were fermented by boiling the juice with a pint of water and a pound of sugar, adding a teaspoonful of yeast nutrient and, when cool, a wine yeast. Additional syrup was then added to bring the gravity up to 90 and it was allowed to ferment to dryness. This wine tasted very rough so another lot of syrup was added and the following table shows how the gravity dropped and how within twelve months a very successful wine was produced.

Date	Gravity
Apr. 30th	130
May 7th	125
July 1st	35
Dec. 7th	21

The wine was racked and remained stable and was bottled in March. It contained 14½ per cent of alcohol and its flavour was similar to port but, of course, it lacked the characteristic body which in port wine is due to the unfermented grape juice retained by the special method of manufacture used in Portugal.

Elderberry and Raisin Wine (Claret type)

It was decided to make a wine from elderberries which would be somewhat like a claret. As this fruit is rather harsh in flavour and a wine produced from elderberries and sugar only is lacking body a formula was devised using equal parts of elderberries and raisins. The following formula will make 4½ gallons.

8 lb. of raisins were minced and brought to the boil in a pressure cooker with 4 pints of water and kept at 10 lb. pressure for 10 minutes. This was fermented for 1 week with a sedimentary wine yeast and the mixture was pressed. To this was added the juice drawn from 8 lb. of elderberries heated with 2 pints of water and pressed. To this mixture 1 oz. of citric acid, 4 teaspoonsful of yeast nutrient, 2 gallons of water and 1 gallon of strong syrup were added. If strong syrup is not to hand 8 lb. of sugar and an additional 4 pints of water can be used instead. The wine will be claret-like on maturing but may require the addition of some more acid and some grape tannin before bottling.

Elderberry Wine, Sweet

The following quantities are sufficient to make about 4½ gallons if the elderberries are full of juice. If not the container is filled up with water to the top later.

 10 lb. elderberries
 2 lb. raisins
 3 lb. sugar
 1 gallon water
 4 teaspoonfuls yeast nutrient
 2 oz. citric acid.

Boil together, cool and add an all purpose or port wine yeast brew. Leave in a well-covered container, stone jug or jar, for one week. Press out, transfer to cask and add a cool syrup made from 6 lb. sugar brought to the boil with 6 pints water. Let fermentation subside, then add another 6 lb. sugar with 6 pints of water and stir into bulk. Nearly fill containers to the top and when the foam has settled down fill up to the top with water. Allow the wine to ferment till no more gas passes through the fermentation trap. Then rack, store for another three months and rack again. The wine can be bottled after it has matured for six months.

Gooseberry Wine, Dry

4 lb. of green, unripe gooseberries, 1 lb. of sugar. Pour over this 1 gallon of boiling water. Add 1 teaspoonful of yeast nutrient and when cool an all purpose wine yeast starter. Leave for two or 3 days then press and add 2 lb. sugar to the juice. Ferment to dryness.

Gooseberry Wine, Sweet

This can be made as above but using 6 lb. of ripe fruit to the gallon of boiling water and increasing the total sugar to 5 lb. Alternatively a ready-prepared syrup of gravity 150 can be used. This is made by adding 4 lb. of sugar to 6 pints of water to make a gallon of syrup. 6 lb. of gooseberries are treated with 4 pints of this syrup, a yeast nutrient is added and when cool a wine yeast or a sherry yeast. Ferment for two or three days, press, then add the remainder of the sugar, i.e. $\frac{1}{2}$ gallon, and if a sherry yeast has been used ferment in the presence of air.

Gooseberry Champagne

To make a champagne from gooseberries is quite easy. One gallon of the dry wine is fermented on with the addition of 10 oz. of strong syrup, gravity 300. If it is desired to remove the yeast eventually then a champagne yeast is advocated. If not, a sedimentary wine yeast will prove satisfactory.

Grapefruit Wine

This wine should be made from the juice only of the fruit; by pouring boiling water over the fruit and leaving for 10 to 20 minutes it will peel very easily so that it is not difficult to separate the white felty mass from the fruit. The segments are pounded, some water added and the juice is strained off. To 7 or 8 large grapefruit allow 3–4 lb. of sugar; the bulk is made up to 1 gallon with water and an all purpose wine yeast added. This is then transferred to a gallon jar and fermented to completion. The wine is next tasted and if it is lacking in flavour some of the outer peel of the grapefruit is added to the wine, either in thin strips or grated. The wine should be tasted again after a few days and if sufficiently flavoured, the peel should be removed. Alternatively more may be required.

Loganberry Wine

Loganberries lend themselves well to a richly-coloured table wine or a wine similar to a port wine. Allow from 4 to 6 lb. of loganberries to a gallon of water. For a dry wine add from 3–4 lb. of sugar and for a sweet wine from 5–6 lb. The fruit is heated to draw the juice or boiling water is poured over it. About *half* the sugar is dissolved in this mixture, a yeast nutrient and, after cooling, a wine yeast or port wine yeast is added. After two or three days the pulp is pressed and the rest of the sugar or an equivalent amount of 60 per cent syrup (about 1¼ pints instead of each pound of sugar) is added.

Mulberry Wine

Anyone lucky enough to possess a mulberry tree will be able to make a most attractive wine. This fruit is frequently lacking in acid and this is best added as lemon juice. Pulp fermentation is desirable and some water may be added. The less water the richer the wine will be. For every 10 lb. of fruit allow 3 lb. of sugar and from ½ to ¾ gallon of water. It is desirable to test the adjusted juice for its gravity and add more sugar or syrup according to whether a sweet or dry wine is required. A wine or port yeast may be used with success.

Orange Wine

Orange juice ferments very well provided the peel is not added till the wine has fermented to completion. Many recipes suggest using the whole orange sliced but this produces a very bitter wine. To use the juice without adding water proves rather expensive. The juice is pressed out, strained through a coarse cloth and an equal volume of water is added. The gravity is then taken and an equal amount of syrup of a suitable gravity is added. Oranges may vary considerably in sugar content and hence the gravity will also range over a wide field. The amount of juice per orange will also vary but an average amount for a large sized, thin skinned, juicy orange is about four ounces. It will therefore require twenty oranges to produce half a gallon of juice. This can be used to make one gallon of a sweet wine but half this quantity, that is 2 pints, is sufficient to make a dry wine. A Campden tablet should be added and it will be necessary to adjust the acidity with citric acid. For a dry wine the gravity should be adjusted to 90 and for a sweet wine to 150. A Hock or a Sauterne yeast should be used. When the wine has fermented to completion some grated orange rind is added to give an orange flavour.

Pear Wine

Some quite delightful white wines can be prepared from pears, but as pears lack acid and nutrient, both have to be added. The fruit should be minced and pressed and if the juice is somewhat lacking in tannin then some of the peel may be soaked for a few days in the fermenting juice. Pulp fermentation is not necessary and not particularly conducive to quality. Great care must be taken to avoid contact with air as this will lead to browning of the juice and a Campden tablet must be added. Pears are preferably used for a dry wine and the gravity of the adjusted juice should be about 85–90 to give a light wine, that is, one with a medium alcohol content.

Plum Wine

Plums are not particularly suitable for the production of dry wines so some residual sweetness is desirable. Each variety of plum will tend to give a product with an individual character and some very distinguished wines can be produced particularly if fermented in the absence of air and with a wine yeast. For sherry-like wines fermentation is carried out in the presence of air and with a sherry yeast. Boiling water is poured over the fruit and to 4 lb. of plums ½ gallon of water is sufficient, together with 1 lb. of sugar, 1 tablespoonful of Pectozyme and a suitable yeast. When this has fermented for 3–5 days it is pressed and from 2½ to 3 pints of syrup of gravity 300 are added. After fermenting to completion a little additional syrup may be added if desired, to give the required sweetness. The wine must, of course, be allowed to mature and be racked at least twice at three or four monthly intervals before bottling. Asbestos filtration is advisable.

Raisin Wine

When making wine from dried fruits it is desirable to boil the fruit well with several lots of water so as to get a thorough extraction. The raisins should be well pounded or passed through a very coarse mincer. Half a gallon of boiling water is poured over 2 lb. of raisins, left overnight and then well pressed. The yield will be about 3 pints of a juice of gravity about 100. The pulp is leached again with another half a gallon of boiling water which on pressing will yield a further 4 pints of juice of a gravity between 40 and 50. By adding the two extracts together 7 pints of a juice with a gravity of about 70 are obtained. Some sugar is added to increase this gravity, for instance, about 1½ lb. of sugar will increase the gravity to about 130 and the volume of the wine to 7¾ pints. A juice such as this was fermented with a Tokay yeast, and the gravity drops were as follows:

Date	Gravity
Apr. 30th	130
May 7th	51
May 17th	39
Sept. 19th	25

The wine was racked at this gravity and two Campden tablets added. It was of a very good flavour, matured well and was quite stable, but a little lacking in acid and tannin. Half an ounce of citric acid and two teaspoonsful of grape tannin effected a marked improvement. A similar juice fermented with a sherry yeast in the presence of air became nutty in flavour but fermented rather more slowly.

Raspberry Wine

Raspberries are rather strong in flavour hence are only suitable for the production of a sweet wine in which the raspberry flavour is retained by fermenting in the absence of air and with a wine yeast. Pulp fermentation is carried out for two to three days and the juice is then pressed. An attractive wine can be made as follows:

6 lb. raspberries, 4 pints water, 1 lb. sugar, 1 teaspoonful yeast nutrient. Ferment on skins for 2 or 3 days. Add 1 pint water, 2 pints syrup and ferment to dryness. Sweeten to taste with some strong syrup after the wine has received its second racking.

Rhubarb Wine

The stalks should be gathered in May and can be used to make a dry or sweet white wine, a sparkling champagne type of wine or a sherry-like wine which can be fortified. When making rhubarb wine it is highly desirable to first remove the oxalic acid present. This is done as follows:

Pour 8 pints of boiling water over 6 lb. of red rhubarb stalk, allow to get cold and press. To this add 1 oz. precipitated chalk, mix well and if the juice tastes sour add another $\frac{1}{2}$ oz. Leave two days, after which the clear liquid can be drawn off and the last portion filtered. Alternatively powdered cuttle fish, which is a pure form of chalk, will be found preferable as it is less likely to clog up a filter. Then add citric acid in small amounts until the juice tastes acid; the sweeter the wine is intended to be, the more acid may be added. To this juice add 1 teaspoonful yeast nutrient, $\frac{1}{2}$ lb. sugar and a suitable yeast culture which for a dry or sweet table wine should be a wine yeast. When the fermentation has started add 2 pints of strong syrup. The gravity will be about 100 and the fermentation should proceed as follows:

Date	Gravity
May 29th	100
June 8th	9
June 30th	0·992

The wine was treated with one Campden tablet and racked and then bottled six weeks later.

Rhubarb Champagne

A dry wine was produced as above but a champagne yeast was used. When clear, 6 oz. of strong syrup were added to 1 gallon of the wine and stood in a warm place. If no yeast growth occurs 1 teaspoonful of yeast nutrient should be added and some fresh champagne yeast. Once fermentation has started the wine is bottled in champagne bottles which are stored on their sides in a cool place for 6–8 months. After that the technique for removal of yeast by twisting and gradual inversion of the bottles can be started.

Rhubarb Sherry

To 6 lb. of rhubarb and 1 gallon of water, after removal of oxalic acid as described above, add 3 lb. of sugar, 1 teaspoonful of yeast nutrient and a sherry yeast. When the wine is nearly dry add 2 pints of strong syrup and ferment on. The wine should be fermented in the presence of air.

Other Rhubarb Wines

Rhubarb, like other wines, can be spiced by adding cinnamon, grated lemon peel or orange peel and traces of nutmeg. Many recipes advocate pulp fermentation for a week but this is not necessary and wines made in this way are frequently difficult to clear and require the use of Pectozyme. Sometimes rhubarb ferments rather too slowly; if so the addition of ½ lb. of chopped-up raisins to the gallon will stimulate the fermentation.

Rhubarb wine is frequently used as the basis for a red table wine. This is best done by adding some elderberry juice which has been drawn by heat. The elderberries are covered with water, brought to the boil and pressed. To this is added one dessert-spoonful of gelatine which has been soaked in cold water. The best gelatine to use is Nelson's powdered gelatine and a half teacupful of water should suffice. The juice is allowed to cool and is then filtered. Sufficient is added to the wine to give a bright red colour. It is desirable to store this wine at least a couple of months before racking and then if dry it may be bottled.

Rosehip Wine

This fruit makes an attractive wine if handled as follows. About 1 gallon of boiling water is poured over 4 lb. of hips and 1 lb. of sugar to produce a pulp to which ½ oz. citric acid is added because otherwise it would lack acidity. Fermentation is then carried out on the pulp for 7–10 days, followed by pressing, and from 2–3 pints of strong syrup are added and the wine fermented on. In the absence of air and with a wine yeast a light coloured, slightly sweet wine will result, while with a sherry yeast and fermentation in the presence of air a sherry-like wine will be produced.

Sloe Wine

Sloes are exceedingly bitter and astringent hence a little goes a long way, but the riper they are gathered the lower will be the acid and tannin content. It is sufficient to use 3 lb. of sloes to 1 gallon of boiling water. About 1 lb. of sugar, 1 teaspoonful of yeast nutrient and, after cooling, a wine yeast are added. Fermentation is carried out on the pulp for five to seven days. After pressing another 3 lb. of sugar are added or 4½ pints of strong syrup. This wine will be rough when young but will improve on maturing.

Strawberry Wine

Strawberries are not often used for wine making as the juice frequently fails to ferment well or turns vinegar sour. To prevent spoilage some sulphite should be added at once to the crushed fruit in the proportion of 1 Campden tablet to the gallon unless the fruit is overripe when 2 tablets are indicated. Furthermore, as strawberries lack acid, from quarter to half ounce of citric acid per gallon should be added at the start of the fermentation. To 5 lb. of strawberries add 1 lb. of sugar, $\frac{3}{4}$ gallon of water, 1 table-spoonful of Pectozyme, ferment for two or three days and then press. To each gallon of juice add 3–4 lb. of sugar and ferment on to a sweet wine. The strawberry flavour will not be retained after fermentation but this wine will tend to become sherry-like. A sherry yeast is advocated.

Walnut Wine

Unripe walnuts are frequently used for wine making. Sixty nuts, which must be green and quite soft, are cut into thin slices and about 4 pints of 40 per cent syrup are poured on to them and $\frac{3}{4}$ oz. citric acid and 1 teaspoonful of yeast nutrient are added. A sherry yeast is used and when the fermentation has almost ceased another 4 pints of 60 per cent syrup are added. When the wine has cleared it is drained off from the nuts and matured in air.

FLOWER WINES

Many attractive wines can be made from blossoms. By them-selves the flower heads which are used contain insufficient organic matter to ensure adequate yeast growth and hence a sound fermentation. Therefore various fruits or their juices such as lemons, oranges, raisins and apples and sometimes even cereals are added to the flowers to ensure effective fermentation. Flowers have a distinctive flavour which they confer on the wine and elder flower, coltsfoot and dandelion are firm favourites. One of the faults in making flower wines is that these frequently lack acid and sometimes tannin. Both should be added, the acid prior to the fermentation and the tannin when the wine is finished and prior to bottling. The recipes which follow are for straightforward flower wines. Some wine makers put spices such as cloves or cinnamon into the brew, but it is better to add such spices to the finished wine rather than prior to fermentation as they sometimes hinder the fermentation and frequently spoil the delicate flavour of the wine.

Flower recipes follow a general pattern. The flower heads are boiled or else crushed and boiling water poured over them. If raisins are used they should be well pounded and then soaked in the warm brew for a few days. The mass, which will tend to float up, must be pushed down twice daily to ensure adequate extraction. It is then pressed and sugar, yeast nutrient, a Campden tablet, the required amount of acid and a yeast starter are added.

Broom Wine

Boil 1 gallon of broom flowers in 1 gallon of water, cool and press. Add 4 lb. of sugar which must be completely dissolved and ½ lb. of raisins or the juice of 2 lemons and 2 oranges. A teaspoonful of yeast nutrient will ensure a sound fermentation and either a wine or a sherry yeast can be used. In the former case the fermentation is carried out under a water seal by using a fermentation lock while if a sherry yeast is used some air should be admitted by using an empty fermentation lock lightly plugged with cotton wool only.

Clover Wine

Boil 1 gallon of purple clover blossoms with 1 gallon of water and 3 lb. of sugar, add the juices of 2 oranges and 3 lemons and 1 teaspoonful of yeast nutrient. When cool add a wine yeast starter and leave from three–five days stirring daily. Strain into a jar which is filled up to the brim and insert a fermentation trap. The wine is left till it clears, is then racked and this operation is repeated again two–three months later. The wine should then be ready for bottling.

Coltsfoot Wine

3 pints of coltsfoot flowers are boiled with a gallon of water to which 3 lb. of sugar are added. Add a teaspoonful of yeast nutrient and the juice of 2 oranges and 2 lemons. When cool a wine yeast starter is added and the brew allowed to ferment for three days when the pulp is pressed and the juice strained into a jar which is filled to the top, fitted with a fermentation lock and allowed to ferment to completion. Racking is carried out as for Clover Wine.

Cowslip Wine

To 2 quarts of bruised flower heads add the juice of 5 lemons and 3 pints of boiling water, stand till cool, then strain through coarse cloth, add 2 pints of strong syrup, a teaspoonful of yeast nutrient and a wine yeast.

Dandelion Wine I

To 2 quarts of dandelion heads add a gallon of boiling water and leave for two days. Strain on to 3 lb. of sugar and the juice of 4 oranges. Stir till dissolved, add some citric acid, yeast nutrient and a wine yeast starter and ferment on to a semi-sweet wine.

Dandelion Wine II

A rather richer dandelion wine is prepared as follows:

Pour a gallon of boiling water over a gallon of dandelion heads and leave from three–five days. Strain into a saucepan and dissolve in this mixture 4 lb. of brown sugar, then add from ½ to 1 lb. of bruised raisins and, if a spiced wine is liked, about ½ oz. of root ginger which must be well pounded. Strain when cool, add a yeast nutrient, the juice of 4 lemons and a wine yeast. This wine will be sweet and should be racked at least three times at two or three monthly intervals after it has cleared.

Elderflower Wine (*Sparkling*)

To 3 pints of elderflowers cut from the stalks add a gallon of boiling water and leave for a few days, stirring occasionally. Strain on to 3½ lb. of sugar and the juice of 2 lemons, add a teaspoonful of yeast nutrient and a wine yeast or champagne yeast. This wine will be nearly dry but when it has started to clear and while there is still some sugar present it may prove suitable to convert into a sparkling wine. A bottle containing some of the wine is stood in a warm place and lightly plugged with cotton-wool. If after a week a slight yeast deposit has formed then it is quite safe to transfer all the wine to champagne bottles which are either closed with corks well wired down or by screw caps similar to cider flagons. The bottles are stored on their sides in a cool place and after six months or so should be sparkling and ready to drink. If on the other hand when trying the wine out for its suitability for bottle fermentation a heavy yeast deposit is noted then fermentation must be continued for a few more days or even weeks till there is less sugar in the wine. A further test then should show a smaller yeast deposit in which case the wine can be bottled and complete its fermentation in the bottle. Bottling a wine which shows a heavy deposit will inevitably lead to burst bottles.

Elderflower Wine (*Sweet*)

Just as dandelion wine can be made richer and stronger by the addition of some chopped up raisins so can elderflower be made into a rather sweeter wine and in that case spices are frequently added. For this allow 3½ lb. of demerara sugar, the juice of 2 oranges and 1 lemon, 1 lb. of chopped up raisins, 4 cloves and a teaspoonful of yeast nutrient to a gallon of water. After standing for three–five days during which a fermentation will have been started with a wine yeast or port wine yeast, the pulp is drained from the liquid and well pressed and the fermentation is allowed to go to completion. This wine will be sweet.

There are many other flower wines and they follow the same pattern as those previously described. Golden rod, marigolds, red and white may blossom, pansies, primroses and rose petals are all used to make a wine, but in every case some yeast food such as a fruit juice or dried fruits have to be added. As with all other wines the young wines may easily be harsh in flavour till they have undergone a period of racking and maturing and quality will only ensue by using a wine yeast and following sound methods. If it is desired to make a sweet wine a port wine yeast is advocated, but for semi-sweet or dry wines the ordinary sedimentary wine yeast will lead to satisfactory clarification and facilitate the wine-maker's task as he may be able to bottle a wine which has been matured without having to do any fining or filtration.

HERB AND VARIOUS OTHER WINES

As with flower wines, herb wines are unbalanced in that they lack acid and tannin and both have to be added. Some herb wines are very much in demand as tonics and this applies particularly to nettle wine. Others are very well-spoken of and one of these is parsley wine. Ginger wine is of course very well known to wine makers and wine drinkers.

Birch Wine

Many wine makers who wish to make birch wine are at a loss how to collect the sap; this is not difficult and is done in the spring when a wedge is cut into the bark of the tree and a folded piece of tin is inserted below the wedge. The sap is collected in a jug and is reputed to make a very attractive wine. It is undesirable to tap a tree more than once as the loss of much sap is a strain on the tree. To a gallon of the sap allow the juice of 2 lemons and 2 oranges, 3 lb. of white sugar and ½ lb. of chopped-up raisins. The whole is warmed to dissolve the sugar. When cool yeast nutrient and a wine yeast are added and left to ferment for about a week. The solid matter is removed by straining and the wine is fermented on till it clears after which it has to undergo several rackings to stabilize the wine and improve the flavour.

Ginger Wine

To ½ lb. of chopped up raisins add 2 oz. of crushed root ginger, 3 lb. of sugar and 1 gallon of water. Bring to the boil and when cool add the juice of 2 lemons and 2 oranges. Follow this by a teaspoonful of yeast nutrient and a wine yeast. Fermentation is allowed to proceed for a few days when the liquid is strained off from the raisins and ginger into a gallon jar and allowed to ferment to completion. This wine will be sweet.

Nettle Wine

To 2 quarts of young nettle tops add a gallon of boiling water and simmer for a little while, generally ½ hour suffices. The liquid is strained and then poured over 4 lb. of sugar, ½ oz. of crushed root ginger, the juice of a lemons and 1 teaspoonful of yeast nutrient. A wine yeast starter is added after cooling. This wine will have a very penetrating odour while fermenting but after racking several times will improve tremendously and become a very attractive wine of golden colour.

Oak Leaf Wine

Oak leaves and walnut leaves are used for wine making but here again some added yeast food such as orange or lemon juice is required. To a gallon of oak leaves add a gallon of water, allow 4 lb. of sugar, the juice from 2 lemons and 2 oranges and a wine yeast. When the wine has finished fermenting an attractive flavour can be conferred by adding some grated orange peel.

Parsley Wine

Boil 1 lb. parsley with 1 gallon of water, stand over night and press. Add five lemons, 1½ oz. citric acid, 6 lb. sugar, 2 teaspoonsful of yeast nutrient and make up to 2½ gallons.

Tea Wine

Tea which has become stewed can be used for making wine. To 4 pints of tea add about ½ lb. of well-pulped raisins and 2 lb. of white sugar and dissolve this by heat. When nearly cool add the juice of 2 lemons, a teaspoonful of yeast nutrient and a wine yeast culture.

Walnut Leaf Wine

This is preferably made by adding a handful of walnut leaves to raisin wine while the fermentation is in progress. With a sherry yeast this will make a wine somewhat sherry-like in type with a good astringency.

VEGETABLE WINES

Many vegetables are used for wine making but only a few make a really attractive beverage. Amongst these I would class parsnip, marrow, lettuce and pea pod wine. Many wine makers take a great interest in the production of potato wine and recipes will be given but it must be remembered that potatoes produce an alcohol which contains a proportion of wood spirit and so recipes which also contain other ingredients such as raisins and in which the quantity of potatoes is kept low are preferable.

Beetroot Wine

5 lb. of well-washed beetroots are sliced thinly, dropped into cold water and brought to the boil till soft; they are then strained and from 3–4 lb. of sugar are dissolved in the liquid. Some acid should be added and half an ounce of citric acid per gallon is a suitable quantity. If the wine is desired spiced, ½ dozen cloves and ½ oz. of root ginger and the peel of some lemon and orange may be added when the fermentation has ceased and the wine has started to clear. (Care must be taken not to add any of the white part of

the orange or lemon peel as this will make the wine bitter.) When boiling root vegetables they should be boiled in an open pan so as to remove as much of the flavour as possible. Carrots and mangolds can be used instead of beetroot to give yellow wines, the beetroot wine of course being red. An all purpose wine yeast will be suitable.

Parsnip Wine

Parsnip makes a very nice sherry type of wine, but it is advisable not to boil the parsnips till they become mushy, but to take them off when the vegetable is just soft enough to be pierced with a fork. 4 lb. of parsnips are boiled with a gallon of water to which about an ounce of citric acid has been added. When soft the pulp is pressed and yeast nutrient added, followed by a sherry yeast. As parsnips contain a certain amount of sugar a fermentation will start in the juice without any further additions. From two to four pints of strong syrup are added when the fermentation is at its height so as to produce either a dry or sweet wine. If it is decided to make a sweet wine it is better to add two separate lots of syrup of two pints each allowing the fermentation each time to become really vigorous for a few days rather than adding the four pints at the start. This will ensure a higher alcohol content and a more satisfactory fermentation.

Green Vegetable Wines

Any green vegetable such as spinach or pea pods can be used for wine making; in the case of pea pods a gallon of water is poured over 5 lb. and this is boiled till the pods are tender when they are strained off. The addition of 2½ lb. of sugar, yeast nutrient and wine yeast will suffice to make this into a dry wine. For spinach wine you use 2½ lb. of spinach and 1 lb. of raisins and proceed in a similar manner. In both cases either the juice of 2 or 3 lemons or half an ounce of citric acid should be added to the gallon to confer the necessary acidity on the wine.

Potato Wine

To 2 lb. of potatoes allow 1 lb. of raisins, 2 lb. of demerara sugar, a gallon of water and either a pound of wheat or a pound of barley. Boil all the ingredients together till the potatoes, which have been sliced, are soft. Strain off the solid matter, add 3 lbs. of sugar and ferment with either sherry or madeira yeast. Just as with fruit wines the young vegetable wines may be raw in flavour but on maturing, provided they have been fermented with a suitable wine yeast in the presence of acid and have been adjusted with some grape tannin to give an attractive bitterness, they will become both palatable and potent. Available recipes differ appreciably in their ingredients but it depends chiefly on the skill of the wine maker whether or not the final product is attractive.

CEREAL WINES

Barley Wine

A recipe for barley wine makes use of a pound each of raisins and potatoes, 3 lb. of either white or brown sugar, a pound of pearl barley and a gallon of water. Here again either an ounce of citric acid or the juice of three or four lemons should be added. Barley will make a good sherry, and a sherry yeast is advocated.

Maize Wine

This can be made by a recipe similar to Barley Wine using a pound and a half of crushed maize to a gallon of water and 4½ lb. of sugar, together with the juice of 4 sweet oranges and a lemon. This formula will make a sweet wine and a sauterne or a madeira yeast will confer a very good flavour after adequate maturing.

Malt Wine

This is made from a mixture of 2 lb. of malt extract and 1 lb. of sugar to a gallon of water with sometimes the addition of a pound of honey. It will tend to taste more like beer than a wine and is just as well made into a beer by using a brewers yeast and adding hops.

Rice Wine

Sweetened rice water is often used for making wine in rice-growing countries such as Burma or India and this wine is known as Sake. A good wine can be made by mixing 3 lb. of rice, which should be coarsely crushed, with 3 lb. of sugar and a pound of chopped up raisins. A gallon of hot water, a teaspoonful of yeast nutrient and sufficient acid (about $\frac{3}{4}$ oz. of citric acid) are added, and, after cooling, a sherry yeast. This mixture is kept in the warm for about a week and stirred at intervals. It is then strained through a cheese cloth into a suitable container where a quiet secondary fermentation will take place and the wine will start to clear.

Wheat Wine

To 1 pint of wheat and 2 lb. of raisins add 4 lb. of brown sugar, the juice of 3 oranges and 2 lemons and a gallon of hot water. Add a teaspoonful of yeast nutrient, $\frac{1}{2}$ oz. citric acid, and, after cooling, a wine or sherry yeast can be used for this mixture, which is strained off from the solid matter at the end of a week. Fermentation will continue and a clear wine will finally be obtained.

THE PRODUCTION OF MEAD

Undoubtedly mead is the forerunner of the wine industry and was drunk in this country by the ancient Britons prior to grapes being introduced from Southern Europe. It was usual to serve mead and mead variants at banquets and other festivities and particularly at weddings. For a whole month after the nuptials mead was drunk from which originated the term the 'honeymoon'. Mead is essentially the product of the fermentation of honey diluted with water or of comb washings and it is not difficult to understand how the art of mead making arose and continued to flourish. As well as producing a pleasant and alcoholic drink it was a desirable outlet for gluts of honey. This is an interesting subject on which to speculate; much honey must have been used for sweetening because there was no sugar but the cultivation of bees and the production of honey was mainly regulated by the necessity for beeswax for candles of which large numbers were required for ecclesiastical use. In addition to honey wine a thinner mead tasting like beer was made by adding hops but gradually production of both declined and the art was lost due to the importation of wines from France, Portugal and Spain. It was also found that malt, prepared from barley, could be used for the preparation of a cheaper but equally palatable beer. It is only in recent years that mead production has again been carried out commercially.

There are several varieties of mead which depend for their differences partly on a different alcohol content and partly on the addition of various spices. Such spices were spoken of as *gruits*; they comprised ginger, rosemary, cloves, nutmeg, maize, cinnamon and sometimes orange peel, which can be used collectively or individually; for example, ¼ oz. of cloves and 1½ oz. of cinnamon powder can be added to 10 gallons of brew prior to fermentation. Quite different types of mead are also made by adding fruit juices which stimulate the fermentation and produce meads with varying flavours. Ordinary mead should not contain too much alcohol and about 12 per cent is entirely satisfactory for a dry mead which is meant to be drunk as a table wine. Sack mead is a sweet mead and should contain 14 per cent–15 per cent of alcohol by volume. When spices are added to such a mead it is called Sack Metheglin, but if the mead used is dry then it is known as Metheglin. Pyment is prepared from grape juice sweetened with honey, while the addition of spices to Pyment produces a wine known as Hippocras. Cyser is produced from apple juice sweetened with honey, while Melomel is made from a mixture of various fruit juices sweetened with honey.

Although honey will ferment well, it must be realized that the sugar content of honey from different sources varies and hence the brew should be tested for gravity prior to fermentation.

A liquid honey will produce a juice of a lower gravity than a thick crystalline honey and one may require as much as an extra half pound per gallon to make a wine which has the same starting gravity. This is entirely due to the higher water content of a thin honey than of a thick crystalline one. Experiments have shown that the addition of 3 lb. of thick honey to a gallon of water can produce a juice of a gravity of 105 while 3½ lb. of a thinner honey may only give a gravity of 95. It is possible to ferment a juice containing 6 lb. of honey to the gallon provided a wine yeast of a sedimentary type is used, but if a powder yeast, like Maury Yeast which is sometimes advocated, is employed the brew will not ferment out for some long time and will tend to be very unstable. This may lead to renewed fermentation after bottling.

Adding honey to a measured amount of water, say 3½ lb. to the gallon, may prove more convenient than diluting the honey and making it up to a gallon but it must be remembered that by the former method the bulk will be increased as follows:

Honey to Water	Total Volume of	Specific Gravity
3½ lb. to 1 gallon	1 gallon 1¼ pints	1·095 approx.
3¾ lb. to 1 gallon	1 gallon 2 pints	1·100 approx.
4 lb. to 1 gallon	1 gallon 2¼ pints	1·118 approx.
5 lb. to 1 gallon	1 gallon 2½ pints	1·127 approx.
6 lb. to 1 gallon	1 gallon 3½ pints	1·145 approx.

3 lb. of honey *in* a gallon has a gravity of 1·118 and is equivalent to 4 lb. of honey *to* a gallon of water. Some authorities on mead recommend 3 lb. of honey in a gallon of water for a dry mead and 4 lb. in a gallon for sweet or sack mead but as mentioned above such directions may produce meads rather less strong than required and it is desirable to test the must by hydrometer. Failing this, it is safer to use an extra ½ lb. of honey to each gallon, i.e. 3½ lb. for dry mead and 4½ lb. for a sack mead. If a very heavy sweet

mead is desired then up to 6 lb. of honey can be added to a gallon
of water, but it is desirable to add it in two lots i.e. 4 lb. to 1
gallon and later on 2 lb. allowing the fermentation of the first
brew to reach its peak and as soon as it appears to subside adding
the rest of the honey. Mixing is best done by pouring the brew
from one vessel to another. This aeration will stimulate the yeast
to renewed activity and the subsequent fermentation is thus more
likely to continue in a satisfactory manner. The most satisfactory
yeast for mead making is, as mentioned earlier, a good sedimentary
wine yeast which induces early clarification, or if a sherry-like
mead is wanted a sherry yeast is required.

Just as in making wine from fruit it is important to see that
honey wines are fermented in the presence of sufficient acid and
from $\frac{1}{4}$ to $\frac{1}{2}$ oz. of citric acid can be added to the gallon, but
generally $\frac{1}{4}$ oz. suffices as during fermentation the brew becomes
slightly acid of its own accord. Honey wines should be fermented
with a yeast nutrient as that will help to produce a clear wine
which can be racked from its yeast deposit, always provided a
sedimentary yeast has been used.

One of the most frequent causes of failure in making wine from
honey, in other words in making mead, is the lack of purity of the
honey. Honey contains yeast and vinegar bacteria and unless the
brew is boiled or a sulphite is added then vinegar fermentation
can occur. Sometimes one can notice a vinegar taint at the beginning of fermentation and the mead can be saved by the prompt
addition of some sulphite, that is one or two Campden tablets to
the gallon. Cool slow fermentation produces very fine meads.

Honey is of course a rather expensive ingredient and some
saving can be effected by replacing part of the honey by sugar. If
this is done it is desirable to choose a dark honey, which generally
is also more strongly flavoured, as mead should have a rich honey
colour when finished. Newly fermented meads are paler than they
will be after maturing when a certain amount of oxidation will
have taken place, but it is not desirable to allow a dry mead to
oxidize and darken unduly. Many meads shown at honey shows
are dark and muddy in appearance and are already condemned

on this account. The choice of honey is important, a pale honey such as a clover or a New Zealand honey will give a finer flavoured mead than a darker honey with a predominant flavour. Such honeys should only be used for spiced meads or when mixed with sugar as otherwise the mead maker will be disappointed with the result. The time to start mead making is generally during the summer months, particularly if it is desired to make still table wines because the fermentation can be completed in the autumn to allow the wine to clarify during the cold weather. But if a sparkling mead is prepared fermentation can be started in October, be allowed to proceed slowly thoughout the winter and the second fermentation be started as the days turn warmer.

Some mead makers emphasize the need of soft water, but personally I do not find that this makes any difference to the quality of the product; what is important is to see that sufficient acid is present, that the wine clarifies naturally and that it undergoes several rackings before bottling. Also most meads are very much lacking in tannin and the addition of some walnut leaves or some grape tannin while the mead is maturing is an advantage. An attractive mead can be made by adding the juice of some crab apples to the honey-water mixture and the juice from about a pound of the apples to the gallon honey and water is a suitable quantity. To assist the meadmaker to produce definite types some typical formulae and fermentation rates are described.

Dry Mead

The following tables will show how the fermentation of a mead proceeded in several cases and how the wine was treated.

Dry Mead No. I—Fermentation with a sedimentary Wine Yeast

$3\frac{1}{2}$ lb. of honey was added to a gallon of water, boiled, cooled, one teaspoonful of yeast nutrient, $\frac{3}{4}$ oz. of citric acid and a sedimentary wine yeast added.

Date	Gravity	
Nov. 12	90	Vinegar tang—one Campden tablet was
Nov. 14	82	added

Nov. 16   76 Clearing
Nov. 19   64
Nov. 23   49
Dec. 2   27 Clear
Dec. 24   17 Brought into the warm
Jan. 1   13 Racked
Mar. 1   ·999 Bottled

Dry Mead No. II—Fermentation with a Maury Yeast

Ingredients as above
Nov. 12   90
Nov. 14   86
Nov. 16   66
Nov. 19   47
Nov. 23   23
Dec. 2   11
Dec. 24   11
Jan. 1   11 Racked
Mar. 1   10 Gravity too high for bottling because of
                danger of bottle fermentation.

This mead fermented again during the summer, after which the gravity dropped to 1·000. It was then racked and bottled two months later.

Dry Mead No. III—Fermentation of 3 lb. of dark honey to a gallon of water with a Wine Yeast

Nov. 12   105
Nov. 14   84
Nov. 16   60
Nov. 19   42
Nov. 23   36
Dec. 2   36
Jan. 4   12 Clear. Racked
Mar. 4   0·999 Bottled

The above meads are typical table wines of the Hock type with an alcohol content not exceeding 12 per cent. They will not have vinosity when young but will improve on maturing. The first two wines comply with the instructions laid down by the National Honey Show Ltd. for the award of the Mead Maker's Mazer. As the award is only given for meads made in the previous year the fermentation should be started as early as possible in the year prior to the show. By starting the brew in January in a warm or temperate room the fermentation can be finished in three months and the mead improved and stablized by racking at two or three monthly intervals. It must be bottled at the end of June so as to comply with the regulation of 'two months in bottle prior to submitting the entry'.

Many mead makers prefer a strong mead and this is easily produced by using a greater proportion of honey.

Strong Mead

Mead with an alcohol content of 14 per cent–15 per cent is made by using 5 lb. of honey to 1 gallon of water. The gravity of such a mixture will be about 127. The honey can be added in 2 portions, say 3 lb. to 1 gallon followed by another 2 lb. when the gravity has dropped to nil. The usual additions of acid and yeast nutrient are required. The bulk will be a little more than 1 gallon but the excess 1¼ pints can be fermented in another container and used for filling up. Strong meads are preferably spiced and then they are called *Metheglin*. Two recipes are given for Metheglin.

Metheglin No. I

8–10 lb. of honey
2 gallons of water
A mixture of herbs, such as marjoram, balm, cloves, mace, lemon and orange peel, ginger and cinnamon.

Metheglin No. II. Sweet

12 lb. of honey
2 gallons of water
Some cloves, lemon and orange peel, cinnamon and ginger.

Sack Mead

A strong mead can be made more palatable by sweetening and extra honey can be added at the start of the fermentation—up to 6 lb. of honey to the gallon of water will ferment without trouble provided a sedimentary wine yeast is used. If on the other hand a mead with very high alcohol content is required then even more honey can be used but only by adding the honey in several stages. If a sherry yeast is used and the fermentation carried out with access of air then the Sack Mead will develop some sherry qualities on ageing.

Sack Metheglin

This is produced in the same way as Metheglin by adding spices to the Sack Mead. Very attractive flavours can be conferred by using fresh elderflower or cowslip flower tied in a bag which is suspended in the mead till sufficient flavour has been leached out.

Pyment

This is made in the same way as dry mead but instead of water a grape juice is used and the honey content reduced to 2 lb. or even less per gallon. It is advisable to determine the gravity of the juice and to keep it about 120 so as to make a dessert wine. Early racking at about gravity 40–50 is advocated as this will prevent all the sugar from being fermented out.

Hippocras

Hippocras is produced from Pyment by the addition of spices or *gruits* and an attractive flavour can be produced by allowing ¼ oz.

of cloves and 1½ oz. of cinnamon bark to 10 gallons of mead. These spices are tied into a bag and suspended in the finished mead till the desired amount of flavour has been conferred.

Melomel

As mentioned earlier, Melomel can be made from any fruit or fruit juice to which honey has been added. 4 lb. rosehips are brought to the boil with 1 gallon of water and the pulp pressed. To one gallon of juice is added 4 lb. of honey, acid as required, yeast nutrient and a sherry yeast, the fermentation being carried out in the sherry manner.

Cyser

This can be either dry or sweet and the progress of the fermentation of a dry Cyser is shown here. One pound of crab apples were washed, minced and the juice pressed out and added to a gallon of water which had been brought to the boil with 3 lb. of honey. A teaspoonful of yeast nutrient but only ½ oz. of citric acid was added as the crab apples contained some acid.

Cyser fermented with Crab Apple juice and a sedimentary Wine Yeast

Date	Gravity	
Nov. 12	90	
Nov. 14	74	
Nov. 16	52	
Nov. 19	28	
Nov. 23	12	
Jan. 2	8	Clear, Racked

This mead was racked again two months later and bottled when the gravity had dropped to 0·990.

Sparkling Mead

To render mead sparkling it can be bottled when the gravity has dropped to about 10, thus allowing the fermentation to complete in the bottle. Alternatively the mead is fermented to dryness, 5 oz. of strong syrup is added to each gallon and then bottled. If it is desired to remove the yeast sediment, the dry mead should be made with a champagne yeast as that has less tendency to stick to the bottle and can be shaken down on to the cork. If on the other hand the wine is to be served without removing the yeast then a sedimentary wine yeast gives the best results as it will remain adherent to the bottom of the bottle and will not float up.

THE PRODUCTION OF PERRY

Perry is obtained by fermenting the juice of pears to either a dry or sweet sparkling beverage. It is not a wine but is akin to cider, being a natural fermentation of an indigenous fruit juice without added sugar; consequently it is low in alcohol compared with a wine. It should be pale golden yellow in colour, clear and well balanced in acid and tannin. This balance is best obtained by using perry pears as culinary pears are far too mild in flavour but, if only eating pears are available, a certain amount of tannin can be added as grape tannin or by adding some of the peel of the pear to the fermenting juice. Pears are rather lacking in yeast food and two teaspoonsful of yeast nutrient should be added to each gallon of juice. It is also advisable to add a Campden tablet and to carry out the fermentation with a champagne yeast. Pears frequently contain a fair amount of sugar and a gravity of 70 is not unusual. This will cause the perry to be high in alcohol if all the sugar is allowed to ferment out, but as a sweet perry is more attractive, fermentation should be stopped while there is still sugar left. This is best done by racking, that is, drawing off from the yeast deposit, when the gravity has dropped by one quarter or one third. If the fermentation is rapid, racking should be done earlier, while with a slower fermenting juice racking should be later. A suitable gravity for a finished sweet perry is 25. Say, for instance, the gravity of the juice was 60, when this has dropped to 45, if the fermentation is vigorous, the juice is racked; if it is slow then the juice is racked at 40. If *very* slow, then racking can be delayed till the gravity is 30. A renewed fermentation will take place and a second racking is carried out at 25. If the perry does not throw a heavy yeast deposit when tried out in a half-full bottle and stored at 65° to 75° F. then it can be bottled in champagne bottles or screw top bottles and stored in a cold place to mature.

If the pears are lacking in acid this has to be added and half to two thirds of an ounce of citric acid is suitable. If it is desired to make a champagne perry which will be more like a wine, then 1 lb. of sugar can be added to each gallon of pear juice before it is fermented. The perry should be allowed to go dry and a further addition of 3 oz. of strong syrup to one gallon of perry and one teaspoonful of yeast nutrient should suffice to render the perry sparkling. The perry is bottled as soon as there are signs of fermentation and the perry will become sparkling.

Perry can be matured and stored in casks but if so these should be as small as possible, kept full all the time and once they are tapped the perry should be consumed quickly or all or part of it should be bottled.

THE PRODUCTION OF CIDER

Cider is a fermented beverage obtained from the juice of apples which have been minced and pressed out in a fruit press. Although any variety of apple can be used, the quality depends very much on the proper blending of certain definite types. Some apples contain much acid and are low in tannin content, amongst these being cooking apples like Bramley Seedling and such apples are called sharp. Another type of apple will have both high acid and and tannin content; these are known as bitter sharp. An apple type very useful in cider making is known as Bitter Sweet and amongst these are the Crab apples. They are low in acid content but very high in tannin. Dessert apples are known as sweet and are low in both tannin and acid content. To obtain a well-balanced cider which will ferment to a reasonable alcohol content it is desirable to have sufficient sugar, acid and tannin present and this can be done by blending sweet and bitter sharp apples or bitter sweet and sharp apples. Blends are generally a matter of choice but usually two parts of medium sharp apples require about one part of sweet and one part of bitter sweet or two parts of slightly bitter sweet apples. If the sharp apple is of the cooking variety then only one part of the sharp apple is mixed with the sweet and bitter sweet as suggested above.

Although unripe apples can and are being used for cider making, the cider will tend to be thin and unattractive and to obtain quality only ripe fruit should be used. The fruit should be allowed to lie in heaps for a couple of days till the apples soften a little as this will facilitate juice extraction and increase the yield. Then it should be washed prior to mincing and it is desirable to test the gravity of the expressed juice and if necessary increase it to about 60. A yeast nutrient is not needed for cider but the addition of one Campden tablet per gallon is a safeguard and a sedimentary wine yeast or a champagne yeast will ensure quality in the product which cannot be obtained if the fermentation is allowed to start of its own accord with the wild yeast which may be present.

Dry Cider

Cider can be fermented to dryness and many cider lovers consider that only dry ciders are worth drinking. It is not desirable to let the fermentation proceed to dryness without any racking as if racking is delayed till all the fermentation has ceased, the quality of the cider will suffer. If a cider that has finished fermentation is racked, most of the gas will be lost, the cider will become still and will have no chance of becoming sparkling; in addition it will have remained unduly long on the lees, which will tend to spoil the flavour. On the other hand if the cider is racked while still sweet it will be removed from most of its lees and any new yeast deposit will use up the remainder of the yeast food and help to make the cider stable. Racking can be carried out at 10 degrees of gravity, or even at 5 degrees, but no lower than that; the cider will then continue to ferment to dryness and will become sparkling.

Sweet Cider

To produce a sweet cider is somewhat more difficult. One can of course add sugar or syrup to a dry cider but this must only be done immediately prior to consumption as otherwise renewed fermentation can take place when the sugar will be converted into alcohol and an apple wine will result. On the other hand, if the cider is racked when the gravity has dropped by only 10 degrees, a renewed slow fermentation will take place and the resulting cider should be sweet with a gravity of about 25, when it will require racking again. But some juices ferment so vigorously that a second racking may have to take place when the gravity has dropped by another 10 degrees, that is a total of 20 degrees. Once the gravity has been reduced to 25 the cider should be again removed from its yeast deposit. If the cider is then bottled some fresh slight fermentation will take place to render it sparkling. One of the difficulties in cider production is a pronounced haze but a cider fermented in the presence of sulphur dioxide, a yeast nutrient and a sedimentary wine yeast will generally clear long before the gravity has dropped to 25. If not, the cider can be rendered brilliant by filtering with the aid of asbestos pulp. Just as immature wines taste raw and unattractive so do ciders which have not undergone a period of maturing. If cider is made in casks it is racked from the deposit as outlined above and left to mature in the cask during the winter. Such ciders are normally bottled in March or April and left for another three to six months to condition in bottle. To prevent burst bottles, a test should be carried out so as to determine how much yeast deposit will be formed during storage. Bottles are filled about three-quarters full with cider, well corked and left in a warm place for 10 to 14 days. If after this period the yeast deposit is only small and the cider sparkling, then it is safe to be bottled, but if the yeast deposit is heavy and much gas is present then the cider must be left to mature for another month or so and again tested for its suitability for bottling. When bottling a syphon should be used or if the cider is drawn from a tap a piece of rubber tubing should be fitted to the tap end which will be long enough to reach down to the bottom of the bottles. By filling slowly and not allowing the cider to splash into the bottles much gas is retained and the cooler the temperature the better will be the retention. If the bottles are corked then these have to be wired into position and the bottles laid on their sides but with screw stoppered bottles with a sound rubber washer there should be no losses of gas and these may be stored upright. Just as in wine making, attention to cleanliness is important and all metals should be avoided as far as possible. Ciders should retain their apple flavour and be quite different from an apple wine; this is possible because they are not fermented so fully, contain less alcohol and do not undergo the same amount of racking and renewed fermentation after racking.

Cider troubles

Cider, like wine, can undergo acetification, grow flowers of wine, or darken. This should not happen if the apples were sound and well washed, a wine yeast and sulphite were used and the containers kept full and protected from air. If troubles occur the remedies are the same as those applied to wines.

HOME BREWING OF BEER

The production of beer and beer-like beverages was, prior to April 1963, not legal without an Excise Licence. Nevertheless home brewing in small quantities, as a more or less experimental exercise, was carried out by quite a few enterprising spirits, especially as there was little enthusiasm to supply licences to home brewers. Fortunately for the art of home brewing the Chancellor of the Exchequer has recognized this somewhat anomalous position by allowing home brewing without a licence or the payment of Excise Duty. Needless to say, the restriction that such brews may not be sold is similar to the one applying to home-made wines. Since the lifting of the ban on home production of beer there has been much interest in and a great demand for up-to-date knowledge on this subject.

Beer making though vastly quicker than wine making presents quite a few problems. The time factor in production and storage can be vital and, unlike wines, the beer does not improve with prolonged storage.

For those who wish to make as good a beer as possible a brief description is given herewith which explains the principles involved in commercial brewing and is then followed by recipes which can be used as an alternative and simpler method for the production of a similar product.

What is beer? The beer of commerce is normally produced from a liquid called wort and this wort is obtained from barley which has been made to sprout and has undergone a subsequent period of drying. This is termed malt. When barley sprouts enzymes are produced which convert much of the starch in the grain into sugar. This sugar is extracted from the sprouted and dried barley, now called malt, by leaching it out with warm water. The resulting liquid, called wort, is used for making beer. Obviously, as wort is obtained by extracting the malt with water, malt extract can be also used for the production of beer. The malt extract which we buy is in fact produced by sprouting barley, extracting it and evaporating off the water to get a thick syrupy product. Such evaporation has to be done at low temperatures under vacuum as the extract would otherwise be spoiled; this cannot be done by an amateur and explains why malt extract is comparatively expensive. While entirely suitable for beer making, beers made solely from malt extract lack a little body so some rice or other cereal is usually added.

The difference between wine and beer is that wine is produced from a liquid consisting of sugar in or added to fruit juices but having comparatively little yeast food, while beer is made from a liquid which consists mainly of grains and starchy matter which under the action of malt is converted into sugar. The wort is very rich in yeast food and any yeast added to the beer will soon grow a heavy crop and cause a vigorous, bubbling fermentation. In wines it is usual to start from gravities well above 70 and generally about 90 or more, while in beers the gravities are much lower, ranging between 30 and 60. The home brewer does not have to make his own malt by sprouting barley as it is easily obtainable now as dried malt from suppliers of wine-making goods.

Malted Grains used in Beer Production

Malts vary in colour and origin. Wheaten malt is very pale and is used in small quantities to give better head retention. The malt which is used predominantly in beer making is barley malt and the colour ranges from very pale to the darkest of chocolate malt. The colour is due to the heating that the malt has received after drying and the darker the malt the less is its diastatic or starch converting capacity. The darker malts are used to give extra colour or flavour but can only be used in conjunction with barley malt, or in the case of home-brewed beer, with malt extract which is high in diastatic value. Blended malts are now available which have adequate starch conversion ability, confer good flavour and colour and are particularly effective in the retention of foam. It is not possible to make a full bodied beer from malt extract and sugar alone. Cereals of some kind are needed and such additions are made by using either flaked maize or ground rice. Such cereals are called grits and are used at the rate of 4 oz. to the gallon and they have to be brought to the boil, preferably in a pressure cooker, so as to gelatinize the starch. After cooling sufficiently for the temperature of the entire brew to be at about 160–170° F. the starch is acted upon by the malt extract until there is no further starch present when tested by iodine. A small sample is removed from the brew to which a few drops of Tincture of Iodine are added. If starch is present the sample will assume a dark blue colour. The entire brew is then brought to the boil with hops and when cooled to about 68° F. (20° C.) the yeast energizer, citric acid, salt and a beer yeast are added. The brew will now contain, besides the malt sugars in the malt extract and the sugar which may have been added, the malt sugar liberated from the cereals and, what is most important, substances known as dextrins. These are starch-like bodies and confer a certain richness to the beer often described as body. These grits are often used in beer production from malted barley too as they prove cheaper than the malted grain.

Hops are normally boiled in the water together with the malt extract and sugar, or added to the boil after the barley has been digested with warm water. As it is desirable to boil malt and the hops together for a while some of the flavour from the hops and some of the volatile oils are lost. To overcome this it is a good idea to keep some of the hops back and only add them to the brew after removing it from the source of heat.

Composition and Gravities of Commercial Beers

	Malt Barley per gallon	Hops in oz. per gallon	Gravity	Approx. Alcohol
Pale Ale	2 lb.	¾–1	55	6%
„ „	1 lb. 12 oz.	½–¾	48	5%
„ „	1 lb. 8 oz.	¼–½	40	4¼%
Light Ale	1 lb. 2 oz. to 1 lb. 4 oz.	¼	32–35	3½%
Strong Ale	2 lb. 8 oz.	1–2	70	8%
Stout	1 lb. 4 oz. to 1 lb. 10 oz.	½–¾	35–45	3½–4½%

When using malt extract the minimum required is ½ lb. to the gallon together with 1 lb. of sugar, and such a beer will be somewhat like a lager beer. For fuller bodied beers more malt or/and additional cereals are needed.

Beer making processes

Several processes of beer making will be outlined here. The brewer who makes beer from malt must exercise rigorous temperature control. If malt has been dried at too high a temperature the enzymes which convert the starch in the grain will have been inactivated and therefore the extract will be low in sugar. If the malt has been dried at the proper temperature it is still possible to spoil the beer by extracting the malt with water at too high a temperature. Before extraction malt has to be ground to a fine grain but not to a powder as otherwise the powder will be difficult to extract and tend to clog up. The malt can be placed on some butter muslin resting in a colander and water at the right temperature poured through it preferably from the fine rose of a watering can. The brewer who uses malt extract and grain mashes (obtained by boiling a cereal like rice or maize or barley in a pressure cooker and straining) is up against fewer difficulties than if he uses malt and will find beer brewing quite simple. He can even do the job without malt extract and a very good beer can be made from bran and brown sugar only. All beers are flavoured by the addition of hops, 1 or 2 oz. or more being added to each gallon of the brew. This helps to give the beer both flavour and stability as hops have preservative properties. In beer making, as in wine making, the use of the right yeast affects the resulting quality immeasurably. Brewer's yeast is generally a top yeast and the brewer has to use certain techniques to remove his yeast which are not available to amateurs. A home brewer is far better served with a Lager beer yeast, as this is a bottom yeast and being sedimentary will enable the beer to clarify and be racked without trouble. For the convenience of home brewers a Lager yeast, Saccharomyces Carlsbergensis, is available as a tube culture and as a liquid yeast.[1] Always remember before adding the yeast that the beer must be cooled to 68° F. (20° C.) and a teaspoonful of yeast energizer to the gallon is an advantage. For the same reason that it is necessary in wine making to protect the brew so it is highly desirable to use a

[1] Obtainable from Grey Owl Laboratories Ltd., Kingswood, Bristol.

fermentation trap when making beer. Futhermore, it is important to have clean barrels and to use a proper beer yeast to prevent acetification or similar troubles. As all beers are brewed with hops they are rather less likely to encounter spoilage than wines, as hops have definite preservative properties besides conferring the desired bitterness on the beer.

Primary and Secondary fermentation in brewing

Just as in wine making there are several fermentation stages, so one can speak in brewing of a primary and a secondary fermentation. The primary fermentation is bubbling and vigorous and will generally be complete in about a week. Starting from an original gravity of about 40 the beer will reach a gravity ranging from just below 1 to round about 4 or 5 degrees. At this stage the beer will generally start to clarify and the yeast and other ingredients such as bran will settle to the bottom. If the beer has been made from malt extract only there will be very little deposit apart from the copious yeast lees and it is possible to rack off nearly all the beer into a jug or other container. The gravity must now be determined and if it is around or below 1, then 1–1½ oz. of sugar or priming finings[1] are added to each gallon. This sugar addition is called priming and will be the cause of renewed fermentation in the bottle. This is called *conditioning the beer*. If the gravity is above 5 and below 10 the beer can be bottled without the addition of sugar as there is still enough sugar present to give the beer a head. At once after the beer has been primed it must be bottled into screw cap bottles and tested after two or three weeks' interval to see whether it is foamy enough. If there appears to be little pressure in the bottle when loosening the stopper, then the stopper must be tightened at once and the beer left for a few more weeks before trying again.

[1] Obtainable from Grey Owl Laboratories Ltd., Kingswood, Bristol.

Testing the Beer for Sugar Content

It is possible to ascertain with quite a degree of certainty at which stage to add the finings or alternatively to bottle the beer without sugar addition. By the use of a Clinitest the sugar content, if below 2 per cent, can be ascertained with the utmost ease. The outfits are obtainable from most chemists and are used by diabetics. Five drops of the beer are mixed with 10 drops of water in the test tube which is provided, using the dropper supplied with the outfit. Next a Clinitest tablet is dropped into the test tube and after 30 seconds the colour is compared with a colour chart supplied with the outfit. If it is bright orange then no sugar is present, if in various shades of green, the corresponding colour on the chart will give the sugar content. It is quite safe to bottle at ½ per cent and this compares approximately with the addition of 1 teaspoonful of sugar to the pint. With this sugar content the beer, if opened as soon as a good head is present, will sometimes retain a little sweetness and be very pleasant on the palate.

Malting of Barley

To convert barley into malt the following procedure should be adopted. Soak barley for three days in water keeping the grain just covered, then drain and place in a heap in a warm place, such as an airing cupboard of which the temperature should preferably be around 15° C. After a few days the barley will start to sprout. It is desirable to turn the heap occasionally so that uniform sprouting takes place. When the sprouts are about half the length of the grain the barley has to be dried. It is extremely important not to dry above 60°C. as above this temperature the enzymes in the malt will be killed. These enzymes are required to convert the starchy matter, some of which remains unchanged in the barley, into sugar. It is necessary to dry the malt so as to make it friable, to arrest any further changes which would carry on while the malt is in a moist condition and to give flavour and colour to the beer.

Producing Beer from Malt

For beer making allow about 1 lb. of malted grain and 1 lb. of sugar to a gallon of water. The malted grain can be either extracted by having water poured over it at 70° C. or it can be soaked in the required amount of water and allowed to stand at that temperature overnight. The malt is then strained off and the liquid is brought to the boil with the sugar and 1 or 2 oz. of hops. As some of the hop flavour is lost by this vigorous boiling, frequently only half the hops are used during the vigorous boil and the remainder added to the brew whilst it is cooling. This wort is allowed to cool to room temperature and is then strained into gallon jars. A culture of lager beer yeast is next added and the container closed with a fermentation trap. When the beer has brewed for about a week it will be nearly dry and should start to clarify when it may be racked. If the gravity is below 1, it is then primed by the addition of 1½ to 2 oz. of syrup of a gravity of 300 to each gallon of brew.

Provided the beer has practically stopped fermenting this amount of syrup may be added without fear but if there are still signs of fermentation then the amounts of syrup suggested are excessive. The beer is syphoned straight into bottles which are immediately closed and left to condition, that is, to undergo a second fermentation and become charged with gas.

Malt and Grain Beers

As mentioned previously the enzymes of malt act on the starch in the barley grain and convert this into sugar. But if desired a saving can be effected in beer brewing by adding some other starchy matter and letting the malt act on this and produce extra sugar. This principle is made use of in the following recipe but to obtain the best results strict attention must be paid to the conditions and particularly to the temperature at which the malt exerts its activity. To make about 2 gallons of beer one needs to soak 1½ lb. of crushed malt (sprouted dried barley grains) in half a gallon of water at 38° C. The mixture is stirred for 10 minutes and kept at 30° C. for another 50 minutes. In another vessel add ¾ lb. of crushed maize or ½ lb. coarse ground rice to ¼ lb. malt in ½ gallon of water. Bring this up to 45° C. and hold it at this temperature for 35 minutes, then bring to the boil and boil for 15 minutes. Mix the two brews together with stirring and bring the temperature up to 72° C. A few drops of the liquid are taken out at intervals and put into a white cup and a drop of iodine solution is added. (Use medicinal tincture of iodine to which an equal volume of water has been added.) At first a blue colour will develop which shows that there is still starch present. When all the starch has been converted into sugar then the iodine solution will not give a blue colour. As soon as this point is reached the brew is heated to 75° C. After this it must be allowed to settle: when clear the supernatant liquid can be run off and the residue is then washed with water to make up the volume to 2½ gallons. Hops are added according to taste, generally from 2–3 oz., and the mixture boiled for a couple of hours. It is then strained, cooled, inoculated with a yeast starter and allowed to ferment to a beer in the normal manner.

Many beer recipes are given which use quite considerable quantities of water and this may present practical difficulties to the brewer. There is no reason whatsoever why the ingredients such as sugar, hops, malt extract or cereals should not be boiled in less water than directed, i.e. in a rather more concentrated form and after straining adding the remaining water direct to the hop brew and this suggestion has been adopted in the following recipe:

Beer from Malt Extract

Boil 1 lb. malt extract with 1 lb. of sugar, 1 oz. hops and 4 pints of water for half an hour, strain and pour another 4 pints of water through the pulp in the strainer to make a gallon of brew. When this has cooled to blood heat a yeast starter should be added, but it will be quite safe to leave it for 24 hours while the starter is being prepared provided the jar is kept closed with a fermentation trap.

The brew should be free from injurious micro-organisms because of the heating it has undergone. The starter is prepared by adding about half a pint of the brew to the yeast in the bottle and standing in a warm place. Vigorous fermentation should ensue within 24 hours and the liquid with its yeast is then poured off into the bulk of the malt brew. This beer will go dry in about a week when it can be racked. It will be a little thin and can be made more attractive by boiling about 1 oz. of rice in a little water in a pressure cooker and adding this prior to the fermentation. After racking, from 1½–2 oz. of strong syrup of gravity 300 are added. The brew is then bottled and a secondary fermentation will ensue in a week or so. The beer will clarify and become sparkling.

Beer produced from Bran, Wheat or Rice

Boil together 1 lb. of sugar, 1 oz. hops, 8 oz. bran or wheat or 2 oz. rice for an hour with 4 pints of water, strain the liquid and pour another 4 pints of water through the strainer. If possible a dark brown sugar should be used or the liquid can be coloured with a little gravy browning. Some of this brew is again used to prepare half a pint of yeast starter which in due course is returned to the bulk of the brew. An improved flavour will be obtained if 8 oz. of malt extract is used to replace 4 oz. of the sugar.

Both the above recipes will give a brew of a gravity about 35 and produce a beer of medium alcohol content. Subsequent addition of syrup will of course make the beer slightly stronger but not enough to make it unduly so. The warmer the beer is kept the quicker will it mature ready for consumption. Many beer drinkers consider that a beer should be ready for use 14 days after bottling. Some prefer to leave their beer in casks but there is some danger of the beer becoming flat and sour and so it is always preferable to bottle all the beer brewed and once a bottle is opened to empty it within a matter of a day or so.

Light Ale

In this example the beer is not primed but racked and bottled while there is still some sugar present. The beer will then go dry and effervescent during storage in the bottle.

3 oz. hops
1¾ lb. brown malt
1½ oz. crushed barley
1½ lb. brown sugar
5 gals. water

Boil the hops, malt and barley for 30 minutes, strain on to sugar, allow to cool to lukewarm and add a Lager Beer Yeast brew. Cover and allow to ferment for about 48 hours till it drops to a gravity of 8. Bottle without disturbing the sediment. This beer can be drunk after five days but improves with keeping.

Strong Ale

3 oz. hops
2 lb. brown malt
2 oz. crushed barley
4 lb. brown sugar
5 gals. water

The strong ale is produced in the same way as the Light Ale but the fermentation and the conditioning will take longer. Again a Lager Beer Yeast should be used.

Many brewers prefer to use honey instead of sugar for beer making. As honey contains a certain amount of water about half as much again of honey should be used to replace the sugar given above. It must be emphasized, though, that honey frequently contains vinegar bacteria and great care must be taken to boil the honey thoroughly before using the brew for beer making.

There are a number of beer-like beverages made in agricultural districts which are reputed to have therapeutic qualities. These include beers produced from dandelion, horehound and gentian, nettle and treacle, while ginger beer is often used as a digestive. These beers are generally made without hops and the following recipes may prove of interest.

Dandelion Beer

Boil ½ lb. of young dandelion plants which have been washed well to free the roots from soil, with 1 lb. of demerara sugar, ½ oz. of ginger root, the juice and the rind of 1 lemon and 1 oz. of cream of tartar for 5 or 10 minutes in a gallon of water. If a gallon pan is not available boil with 4 pints of water and add the other 4 pints after straining. When cool add a beer yeast, insert a fermentation trap, allow it to work till nearly dry and then draw off into strong screw-stoppered beer bottles.

Nettle Beer

Wash 2 lb. young nettle tops and boil in 4 pints of water for 15 minutes and strain, add to this the juice and the rind of 2 lemons, 1 oz. cream of tartar and 1 lb. of brown sugar and another 3 pints of water. Transfer the brew to a gallon jar, add a lager yeast starter, close the gallon jar with a fermentation trap and allow to work until nearly dry. Rack and transfer to beer bottles and keep for a week or so before drinking.

Treacle Ale

1 lb. of golden syrup and half a pound of black treacle are brought to the boil with 4 pints of water, strained, a yeast culture is added, and treated as above.

Ginger Beer

To 1 oz. of root ginger, ½ oz. cream of tartar, the juice and rind of 1 lemon add 1 lb. of sugar and 4 pints of water, bring to the boil, strain, then add another 4 pints of water and a yeast culture.

This formula may not ferment very well as there is insufficient yeast food present and in that case will remain over-sweet. It is preferable therefore to add say a pound of raisins to the above recipe and only half a pound of sugar instead of a pound.

ℰ5℈

Miscellaneous Wine Making Information

Laws affecting the production of Wine and its Sale

All fermented beverages with the exception of perry and cider are subject to Excise control and the levelling of Excise duty if such beverages are offered for sale. Anyone may make wine for their own consumption and even may use such wine as gifts but if it is intended to sell the wine then it can only be produced under the control of the Excise Officer. Wines are known by the Customs and Excise as 'Sweets' and to make sweets a 'Sweets-makers' Licence' has to be acquired at a cost of five guineas annually. Premises and equipment must be segregated, plainly marked and open to inspection by the Excise Officer at all times. All the wine which is made will become dutiable even if used for home consumption. Records have to be kept and are inspected and a weekly declaration has to be sent to the Excise Officer to declare whether wine has been sold or not. Duty is paid weekly but by agreement may be paid monthly.

Duty on British Wine

The present rates of duty per gallon for British wines sent out from a winery for consumption in Great Britain are as follows:

Light wines	Other wines
(up to 27 per cent proof)	
Still 17s. 9d. per gallon.	Still 19s. 9d. per gallon.
Sparkling 23s. 9d. per gallon.	Sparkling 25s. 9d. per gallon.

26. Blue Portuguese Vine, fruit setting early in July. Prolific and early

27. Three stages in the development of fruit on outdoor vine. *Right:* young before the bunch turns down. *Left:* as the bunch turns over. *Centre:* early September but not yet ripe

29. Bunch of grapes after thinning

28. Greenhouse grapes, bunches prior to thinning

Wines may also be fortified and for this purpose a permit can be obtained for duty free spirit but fortification can only be carried out in a bonded warehouse or room which is kept locked and in the presence of the Excise Officer. It takes time to get permission to fortify and the Customs and Excise insist on a bond being taken out by the wine maker who wishes to fortify his wine.

After the wine has been made it is absolutely essential that it is analysed for its alcohol content. The labelling of wines is extremely strict and as the amount of alcohol has to be declared the wine maker cannot afford any mistakes. If the wine contains less alcohol than the declaration he will fall foul of the Public Analyst for selling a substance not of the nature as declared by the label, while if it contained more than the permissible amount then the wine maker will be in trouble with his Excise Office for underpaying of duty. Furthermore only wines made from grapes and in the country where the grapes are grown may be labelled as wine. If the grapes are imported or if grape concentrate is used then it must be called British wine. While if other ingredients are used then the ingredients have to be clearly specified on the label.

As emphasized above a wine maker making wine for sale has to have a licence; this also entitles him to sell wine, but the smallest quantity he may sell to any one person is two gallons, that is one dozen bottles but there is no upper limit to the quantity he may sell. If he wishes to sell in quantities of less than one gallon he has to apply to a magistrate for a retail licence.

Labelling of Wines

The labelling of wine is controlled by the Labelling of Food Order No. 2169 which lays down that wines not made from grapes must be labelled as follows:

'In so far as a wine is derived from fruit, not grapes, the lable must state the fruit or fruits used as a prefix to the word wine in letters the same dimensions, i.e. Apple Wine or Orange Wine. The amount of alcohol must also be declared as percentage proof spirit or per cent of alcohol by volume. The fruit used must be declared also in the following form:

> Fruit Basis Exclusively (X)
> Not less than (Y)

Where X is the fruit and Y is the percentage of alcohol or proof spirit.

If more than one fruit is used the following declaration applies:

> Fruit Basis (X1) and (X2)
> Not less than (Y)

Fruits include rhubarb. Where fruits are not used, as for instance in wines made from honey, the label must declare this as follows:

> Not made from fruit
> Not less than (Y)

Wines made from indigenous-grown grapes could, according to the labelling law, be simply labelled as wines but such a procedure would be unusual. If wine is made from imported grape juice then the prefix to the wine must state the country of manufacture e.g. British Sherry. Geographical names which are not names of distinctive types shall not be applied to liquor (in other words wine) produced in any locality other than the particular locality indicated by the name.

Although not mentioned in the Labelling Order, the word Port is not allowed to be used in England even with the prefix British. This was agreed to in an Anglo-Portuguese Trade Agreement and in England the words 'Port type' are used. This restriction does not apply in other countries or the colonies.

The Determination of the Acid Content of Wines and Juices

To determine the acid contents of wines and juices a small amount of apparatus and chemicals are required.

These are One 10 mil. Pipette.

One 25 mil. Burette.

One litre of $\frac{n}{14}$ Sodium Hydroxide Solution.

One bottle say 100 mil. of British Drug Houses Universal Indicator.

Distilled Water.

One 100 mil. flask—Preferably an Erlenmeyer Flask.

Proceed as follows: Suck up a little more than 10 mils of the wine into the pipette and let it run down to the mark found near the top end of the pipette. The wine is prevented from flowing out by keeping the forefinger pressed well down on the top of the pipette. Transfer the liquid to the Erlenmeyer flask by letting it run into this, draining the pipette well and blowing out the last drop.

Then add about 20 mil. or more of distilled water and a few drops of Universal Indicator. Fill the Burette with your $\frac{n}{14}$ Sodium Hydroxide solution and run out excess till the solution reaches the first division. Add this solution to your flask carefully. A gradual colour change will be noted and this change gives a clear indication when the end point, a good sage green, is reached. These colour changes and their respective pH values are depicted on the label of the Universal Indicator bottle. The end point is easy to detect in light coloured wines. Red wines have to be partially discolourized by shaking up with charcoal powder and filtering but they can also be titrated without the addition of Universal Indicator as the red pigment changes to purple at the end point.

The acidity is easily recorded as citric acid since each mil. of $\frac{n}{14}$ Sodium Hydroxide records 0·1 per cent of this acid in the wine, i.e. if 10 mils of Sodium Hydroxide are used the acidity will be 1 per cent. If 5 mils are used it will be 0·5 per cent. This holds good if a 10 mil. pipette is used. If 20 mils are titrated with $\frac{n}{14}$ Sodium Hydroxide then each mil. of Hydroxide corresponds to 0·05 per cent. It is useful to remember that if ever the end point is overrun by adding too much Hydroxide or if one wishes to check the accuracy of the first titration all that is required is to add a further 10 mil. of wine or juice to the Erlenmeyer Flask and continue the titration to the neutral green colour.

Universal Indicator is much more reliable and useful than Phenolphthalein solution as it gives a gradual approach to the end point and is not affected by the carbon dioxide present in the air.

Do's—Dont's of Wine Making

Do use sound fruit.

Don't forget to wash your fruit.

Do boil your fruit or add one or two Campden tablets if your fruit is over-ripe or unsound.

Don't use metal containers for fermenting

Do remember to sterilize wooden containers.

Don't forget to wash all utensils.

Do remember to use the right amount of sugar.

Don't forget to test the gravity of the adjusted juice.

Do remember that the gravity of fruit juices varies.

Don't forget to use a suitable wine yeast.

Do remember to add a yeast nutrient to fruit wines.

Don't forget to cover your fermenter during pulp fermentation.

Do insert a fermentation trap.

Don't fill your container full till the vigorous first fermentation has subsided.

Do remember to have some spare wine for filling up.

Don't allow an air space over any wine during secondary fermentation and maturing with the exception of a sherry.

Do give sherry wine plenty of air.

Don't forget that flower wines need fruit juice.

Do remember to add acid where necessary.

Don't add sugar in the solid state, always dissolve in fruit juice or water.

Do remember that adding sugar or syrup at intervals makes for stronger wines.

Don't forget to rack your wine at intervals.

Do top up your fermenter after racking, with water if no spare wine is available.

Don't fine your wine unless it refuses to clarify after several rackings.

Do stir up the yeast deposit to help your wine to clarify.

Don't forget that racking improves wine flavour.

Do remember that wines are stabilized by racking.

Don't bottle your wine till it has been tested for stability.

Do remember to add one or more Campden tablets to wines which darken on standing.

Don't add a Campden tablet to wine which is to become a sherry.

Do remember wine making requires patience.

Don't despair, even poor wines improve on maturing.

TABLE XII

CONVERSION OF DEGREES CENTIGRADE TO DEGREES FAHRENHEIT

Cent.	Fahr.	Cent.	Fahr.
−10	14	21	69·8
− 9	15·8	22	71·6
− 8	17·6	23	73·4
− 7	19·4	24	75·2
− 6	21·2	25	77
− 5	23	26	78·8
− 4	24·8	27	80·6
− 3	26·6	28	82·4
− 2	28·4	29	84·2
− 1	30·2	30	86
0	32	31	87·8
1	33·8	32	89·6
2	35·6	33	91·4
3	37·4	34	93·2
4	39·2	35	95
5	41	36	96·8
6	42·8	37	98·6
7	44·6	38	100·4
8	46·4	39	102·2
9	48·2	40	104
10	50		
11	51·8		
12	53·6		
13	55·4		
14	57·2		
15	59		
16	60·8		
17	62·6		
18	64·4		
19	66·2		
20	68		

TABLE XIII

CONVERSION OF DEGREES FAHRENHEIT TO DEGREES CENTIGRADE

Fahr.	Cent.	Fahr.	Cent.
42	5·55	74	23·33
43	6·11	75	23·89
44	6·67	76	24·44
45	7·22	77	25
46	7·78	78	25·55
47	8·33	79	26·11
48	8·89	80	26·67
49	9·44	81	27·22
50	10	82	27·78
51	10·55	83	28·33
52	11·11	84	28·89
53	11·67	85	29·44
54	12·22	86	30
55	12·78	87	30·55
56	13·33	88	31·11
57	13·89	89	31·67
58	14·44	90	32·22
59	15	91	32·78
60	15·56	92	33·33
61	16·11	93	33·89
62	16·67	94	34·44
63	17·22	95	35
64	17·78	96	35·55
65	18·33	97	36·11
65	18·33	98	36·67
66	18·89	99	37·22
67	19·44	100	37·78
68	20	101	38·33
69	20·55	102	38·89
70	21·11	103	39·44
71	21·67	104	40
72	22·22		
73	22·78		

6

The Cultivation of the Vine

It is not proposed to discuss at length the history of vine cultivation as several books have already been published on this subject. Briefly, the vine is reputed to have been grown in Egypt for wine making as early as 3500 B.C., while about 2000 B.C. it was introduced into Europe and around 280 A.D. brought to Britain by the Romans. There is plenty of evidence that grapes were cultivated for wine making in the southern half of Britain and place names such as Vine Street in London and the Vineyard in many parts of the West Country confirm that grape growing outdoors was quite a common occupation. In fact, up to 1914 wine was produced commercially in Glamorganshire on the estate of the Marquis of Bute at Castle Coch but owing to lack of labour during the war period this vineyard fell into disuse. There are vines still growing wild at Tortworth in Gloucestershire on vineyard terraces reputed to have been built by Roman legionaires stationed there. There is no doubt at all that grapes can be grown successfully for wine making in this country, especially as early ripening hybrids are available nowadays. Many growers are trying out different varieties in small vineyards all over the south of England while vines for sale are being grown outdoors in the north.

To grow grapes successfully, that is to obtain a good crop which ripens well, requires some fundamental knowledge allied to a little experience gained on your own soil which naturally takes a little time. The author has grown about 400 vines of different kinds in a vineyard on Cotswold soil, has visited most of the vineyards of any size in England, has studied vine growing in many countries and by attending several viticultural conferences in Germany. The conclusions reached through such practical experiences are embodied herewith and are aimed to help the reader to grow vines successfully.

VINE SPECIES

European Vines

Some consideration should first be given to the various kinds of vines which are available. The grape vine which is indigenous to Europe is *Vitis Vinifera* while on the American continent there are other varieties grown for wine production. These American vines are extremely vigorous and have certain advantages over the European vine for example, they are more resistant to mildew and are not damaged by the vine louse, which is called phylloxera. This louse, which burrows into the roots of the European vine and eventually kills it, was introduced into Europe by the importation of some of these immune American vines carrying phylloxera and was the cause of vast devastation in European vineyards. In fact the soil of such vineyards became completely useless for growing vines of the European varieties which led to the production of a new kind of vine, namely European vines which were grafted on to American rootstocks. Such vines could be planted into soils which had been exposed to phylloxera and remained immune from attack. Therefore on the Continent the European vines which grow on their own rootstocks are being progressively replaced by grafted varieties. Great Britain, up to date, is free from phylloxera so grafted vines are not necessary here, but as the various rootstocks have different soil requirements it is often an advantage to plant grafted vines which suit a particular soil. Furthermore these American rootstocks confer great vigour on a vine and a certain amount of immunity to mildew, hence on this count they are again preferred to the non-grafted types (see plate 22).

Hybrid vines

In an attempt to produce vines which have the character of European grapes and yet the immunity of the American varieties, a number of European wines were crossed with the American vine *vitis Rupestris* to produce what is known as hybrids. The main research work in this field was carried out in France and the vines are generally known by the name of the breeder followed by a number. They are also known as P.D. vines, which stands for Producteurs Directs or direct bearers. These vines are not as yet adopted in Germany and only to a small extent in France and it may be that it is feared that a vine which crops as heavily as these hybrids may increase the already existing over-production of wine. Anyhow, as regards this country there is much to be said for growing such hybrids as many of them have proved to be prolific, early ripening and resistant to lime and to disease (see plate 23).

As a guide to those importing vines, which is strictly controlled for the purpose of keeping out phylloxera, details are given herewith of the various American rootstocks and their particular suitability to different soils.

AMERICAN GRAPE VARIETIES USED AS GRAFTING ROOTSTOCK FOR EUROPEAN VINES

Vitis Riparia

Is indigenous to the temperate parts of North America and is found mainly on the well-wooded banks of rivers. This vine is completely phylloxera resistant and is not affected by extreme cold. It is deep rooted, prefers soil low in chalk and as it shoots early it may be affected by late frosts but if this is avoided early ripening of the grapes can be expected.

Vitis Berlandieri

Is found only in the hotter south-western regions of North

America such as Texas. It also is resistant to phylloxera but not to cold. This vine prefers soil with a high chalk content and is particularly valuable for grafting purposes as the grafts take easily and the vines mature well and at an early date.

Vitis Rupestris

This vine is particularly useful as it is not only resistant to phylloxera but owing to its lateness of growth there is little to be feared from late frosts. It is indigenous to the southern parts of the United States where it is found in dry and sandy soil. Its resistance to cold is slight and when used for root stock both the grapes and the wood are late in ripening. Widely employed for the production of hybrids.

A variety of crossings are also used for grafting vines and they are as follows:

(1) *Riparia x Rupestris* 3309 *Couderc* (1881)

Is a root stock suited to a well-drained warm soil with a low or medium chalk content (maximum 30 per cent), is very fruitful, not very vigorous in growth but the grapes set well. It is suitable for granite and slatey soil.

(2) *Berlandieri x Riparia Teleki* 8 *B*

Will grow in soils containing up to 50 per cent of chalk and is more vigorous than the previous, even in poor and wet ground. This variety tends to chlorosis and is liable to disease.

(3) *Berlandieri x Ripara Teleki* 8 *B Sel.Kober* 5 *BB*

Commonly known as Teleki 5 BB, is a rootstock widely used in Germany and Switzerland, is suitable for ground with a high chalk content and equally productive in cold and wet clay or loam soils. Teleki 5 BB is very vigorous and fruitful but in deep rich soil it tends to shy setting.

(4) Berlandieri × Riparia Teleki 8 B Sel.Kober 125 AA and 127 BB

Is similar to the foregoing, is easy to graft, particularly with Sylvaner, and the grafts grow vigorously.

(5) Berlandieri × Riparia 161/49 Couderc

Is particularly valuable for dry stony ground with a high chalk content and is resistant to chlorosis.

(6) Berlandieri × Riparia Sel.4 Oppenheim (SO 4)

Is liked for its vigour, early ripening of the wood and good growth when grafted with Sylvaner or Blue Portuguese. Should be used for wet and heavy loam soils provided they contain no more than 25 per cent of soluble chalk. It is resistant to phylloxera and is used preferably as rootstock for Traminer, the Burgundy grape and the Riesling.

These interesting details have been extracted from the German book by Dr. E. Vogt entitled 'Weinbau' which is a mine of information on the grape and its cultivation.

This formidable list should not frighten those wishing to lay down a vineyard nor is it at all necessary to grow only grafted varieties. Anyone ordering vines from abroad will be sent European vines grafted on American rootstock. It is therefore advisable to indicate the type of soil where the vines are to be grown. European and hybrid vines can be bought in England and these are of course not grafted. Those who wish to produce a vineyard at a low cost and are prepared to wait are well advised to plant a variety of vines and propagate from those which do best on their particular soil. Experience in the author's vineyard which has been corroborated by another grower in the south of England is that the Gamay, a vine well spoken of as prolific both in this country and abroad, simply cannot be grown on its own roots on Cotswold soil nor does it thrive when grafted on to a lime resistant stock. In the case of another locality where many

Hybrid Seyve Villard 5/276 are growing and cropping prolifically in a rich but rather close textured soil, the Gamay has also proved a failure. This shows the importance of not ordering too many European vines of one variety at the start but of trying out several kinds. For the same reason it must be emphasized that quick decisions cannot be made and that rule of thumb methods are useless. The vine and its growth has to be studied and the soil understood. For instance, although it is generally held that young vines should not receive nitrogen fertilizer, it has been found that on Cotswold soil intense chlorosis occurs which can be cured by giving liberal doses of ammonium sulphate. Contrary to the general view that this will make for soft sappy growth, such does not result in the Almondsbury Vineyard, but if vines on rich soil are treated with inorganic nitrogen they could easily become unproductive through overstimulation and the production of sappy wood. Therefore with an understanding of the nature of the growth of the vine and of the requirements for obtaining fruiting buds and ripe wood and by the proper choice of vines, outdoor grape growing should be as successful in this country as on the continent.

THE VINE AND ITS GROWTH

All vines are capable of prolific growth, especially in countries where there is much rainfall. Watching a vine put forth its shoots in the spring gives one an insight into the rapid rate a vine can grow. Almost overnight, provided the atmosphere is congenial, a shoot will have altered in size and unfolded its leaves. Left to itself the growth of the vine eventually becomes rank, the shoots and the tendrils become entangled and frequently signs of disease will appear. How is it that the vine is one of the few climbers which can scale trees and in some cases cover the entire side of a house? The answer lies in the fact that the vine has an extensive root system which after some years will burrow deep into the ground. Old vines cannot in fact be dug out but horses and chains have to be used to pull up the plant. This extensive root system exerts a great upward pressure of sap, so much so that one cannot cut any wooden part of a vine once the sap is rising without causing prolific loss of sap, also called bleeding. This ability of vines to grow to high heaven is one of the reasons why the novice complains of lack of fruit on his vines. Anyone who grows fruit trees knows that when there is a great growth of leaf the tree usually lacks fruit. Steps are taken to control this rise in sap such as bark ringing or severe pruning. Now anyone who understands plants will appreciate that undue pruning must weaken a plant as the leaves after all produce the food which nourishes the plant. A balance must therefore be held, that is growth must be restricted to ensure ripe wood but the plant must be well nourished by sufficient leaf. The larger the leaf grows, the bigger will be the resulting bunches. The first leaves formed are always larger than those grown in the axils of the plant, so this is one reason why axillary growth, that is the shoots which sprout between the main stem and the main leaf, should be pinched out as soon as formed. Another and more important reason why this growth should be nipped out as soon as grown is that the fruiting buds are laid down on the stem at the slight thickenings, called nodes, and these buds are deprived of nourishment if axillary growth is allowed. Hence this kind of shoot pruning, called summer pruning is essential to obtain good fruiting. Undue axillary growth can also be caused by faulty pruning or lack of staking for if a young vine is left unsupported then, instead of growing to a great height, it will tend to make axillary growth so as to help to balance the plant. In the first year the vine must be encouraged to grow as tall as possible by tying on to a stake right from the start. A common fault is to stop the growth at a certain height too early in the summer, which again leads to axillary growth and entails much summer pruning. Naturally a certain amount of judgment must be exercised but in general, unless shoots from older vines grow above six feet they should not be cut back till some time in August. After this the rate of axillary shoot production is less intense so it is quite in order, and in fact highly desirable, to shorten the main shoots to between three and four feet. That will give the shoots time to mature and produce well-ripened canes.

Methods of pruning and training a vine will be discussed under the appropriate heading but briefly the vine is made up of a root system and a stem which grows thicker each year but which does not produce fruit. The fruit is borne only on wood of the preceding year which grows out from a bud on the stem, starting as a soft green shoot which grows to considerable length and which hardens in the autumn or winter to a cane. This is the fruiting cane. Vines may range from plants with a very long trunk to those with only a short stem. The long trunk will produce many shoots which will harden to canes. These will be cut back hard to a short length of cane carrying one or two well-grown fruiting buds which are called spurs. This pruning is therefore called spur pruning. If the stem is only short, as is the case with vines grown in the open, then only one or two canes carrying two or more buds are retained for fruiting. This is called cane pruning which may be long, that is carrying many buds, or short, that is carrying only a few. There are a variety of methods of training vines all of which restrict the growth of the plant, for the greater the restriction the better will the fruit ripen.

An interesting case in point is the growing of vines in Portugal. Here two main kinds of wine are produced, port which is made from grapes with a high sugar content and a table wine called Vinho Verde from grapes low in sugar. It has been found even in countries as far south as Portugal that only in very favoured positions do the vines produce sufficient sugar for high quality wines. Therefore only the grapes grown on the sunny hillsides in the Douro Valley are used for port wine production but, just as in other wine growing districts further north, the height of the vines is greatly restricted to encourage a high sugar content. (See plate 26.)

On the other hand anyone travelling through Portugal will be amazed to see how vines are grown in woods, over walls, over trees, over tall granity arches, covering balconies and houses and in every case the grapes are used for the production of wine. But these wines are known as *Vinho Verde* or green wines and some of them are rather acid and low in alcohol; nevertheless they are consumed very extensively in the countryside. An illustration shows how such vines are grown up granite posts about ten feet high, only the tops of the vines being allowed to produce shoots, the stem being kept completely bare (see plate 25). Such tall vines, like those grown over houses or trees (see plate 24), carry a lot of fruit but no one worries unduly if the berries are not very ripe as the resulting rather sour wines are much appreciated locally. It has always been held that the further south you go the higher can the vines be trained but it is extremely interesting to see that in some parts of Spain vines are grown on legs which are only a few inches in height, at the utmost ten inches. Although some of these old vines could easily produce a dozen or more shoots from the top of the stem, even here the number of shoots is restricted to three or four, or at the utmost six are allowed to grow, so as to ensure a high sugar content in the grapes. Obviously as vines require restricting even in warm countries it is still more important to reduce the amount of fruit which is to be carried by a vine in colder countries if adequate ripening is desired.

Outdoor vines normally flower in June. Provided the weather is dry at the time, the fruit should set well. While flowering the bunches are erect but soon after the fruit has set the bunches start to turn down (see plates 26 and 27).

GROWING VINES IN GREENHOUSES

Many wine makers are trying their hand at indoor grape grow-and are looking for guidance on this subject so it was considered desirable to include a section in this book. Vines are easy to grow, but as with everything else some methods are more successful than others and good crops can only be obtained by applying suitable techniques.

Thomas Rivers & Son Ltd.

30. Selection of greenhouse grapes

Black	Appley	Gros
Alicante	Towers	Colmar

Mrs. Prince's	Gros	Madresfield	Muscat of
Black Muscat	Maroc	Court	Alexandria

31. Scheurebe grafted on 5BB. A new crossing of Sylvaner and Riesling Strain No. 88 growing in Almondsbury Vineyard

32. Outdoor grapes hanging after leaf fall, Almondsbury Vineyard

Planting the greenhouse vines

Many amateurs are somewhat worried over the question of planting and training and different views on the best methods are frequently held. At one time it was considered that a vine should have its root outdoors and be brought into the greenhouse through an opening in the wall. This method is still advocated by many growers as it does solve the watering problems but as the roots will run where they like it makes feeding of an indoor vine rather difficult. Many growers advise planting the vine inside the greenhouse in a border which has been cemented out, but sometimes this has led to failure, the vine becoming unhealthy and diseased. It may be as well to examine the reasons why this has been so. If a plant is put into a space of soil which it cannot fill with its roots in a reasonable time the soil will go stagnant and sour and affect the health of the plant. The vine prefers a soil slightly alkaline and if therefore the vine is planted into too large a trough containing good rich soil the roots will not be able to fill it and the soil will become sour. Furthermore planting into a good rich compost would tend to a luxuriant but rather soft leaf growth before a root system had established itself and this might also lead to yellowing and sickness. The art of getting fruit on a vine is to get good hard wood which will ripen early in the winter and in which fruiting buds will be laid down. The first important principle therefore is to plant the vine into soil which is not too rich and which will encourage a sturdy growth. The compost can be mixed with chopped-up turves and builders' rubble and vines planted in such mixture do well. Furthermore adequate drainage must be provided as vines do not survive in stagnant conditions. When planting into a cemented trough the base must be well provided with clinkers and preferably with some drainage pipes. The trough should be only partly filled by building up a section with turves and planting the vine in this restricted space. In a year's time this space will have been filled with roots and a further section of the trough can be filled in with more soil held in position by turves. It is of course possible to fill the entire trough, which has been dug out on one side of the greenhouse, by planting this with several vines and thus preventing unused soil going sour. In that case the training of the vines will be different from that used if only a single one is planted in the trough. Vines are preferably trained out horizontally, but if more than one vine occupies the greenhouse then they have to be trained upwards towards the roof.

Having received the vine from the grower the amateur will be delighted to find this has perhaps from five to seven feet of cane. He will tie this up carefully and expect some fruit in the following year but will frequently be disappointed. Better results are obtained by shortening this long cane by a third when quite likely one or two bunches of grapes will result in the first year of planting. The vines will generally be delivered in the late autumn or early in January. After planting they should not be cut at once but should be allowed a spell of cold in the greenhouse, that is during December and January the greenhouse door should be left open. Vines are very hardy and cold tends to make them more productive by ripening the wood. Newly planted vines should be pruned at the end of January but older vines are best pruned in December.

Training the greenhouse vine

Unless a vinery type of greenhouse is used vines are preferably trained out horizontally. In a proper vinery the roof starts at quite a low level and slopes very gradually. This ensures a very long roof and enables the vines to be trained below the roof at not too great a slope. Also they can be brought down by untying them from their supports and laid on to the ground prior to the rise of sap, or even at pruning time. The vine is a climber and will always produce its best shoots and biggest bunches at the apex of its growth unless the tip of the vine is brought below the horizontal. This encourages even breaking and fruiting. Even canes which are trained out horizontally are best lowered during the winter till all the shoots have grown a few inches. The vine is then tied up to the glass but preferably eighteen inches below it. This will enable the shots to grow towards the light and produce a flower with at least one leaf beyond the flower without touching the glass. At this point, that is about a week after the formation of the flower, the growing point of the shoot is pinched out.

If the vine has not reached its full extension the end shoot is allowed to grow competely unrestricted and even if it is not required for extending the vine it is better not to pinch this shoot at all but to prevent it from touching the glass by drawing it down gently and tying to some lower support. If this extension shoot is stopped during the active growing period, there is likelihood of excessive axillary growth taking place and as far as possible this should be prevented. Any axillary growth should be removed as soon as noticed and provided no leaf has developed it can be pulled off, but once a leaf is unfolded then the shoot should be pinched beyond this first leaf. It is quite safe to cut or break off green foliage during the summer but no wooden part of the vine should be cut after March in the open, or after January in the greenhouse, as the vine will otherwise bleed, and this may easily weaken it. As soon as the vine has produced its blossom then the shoot is pinched after the third leaf beyond each bunch, but small bunches and all adherent tendrils should be removed. When the fruit is beginning to clear and show stones, generally in August, the growth of the extension shoot may be arrested by pinching out the growing point.

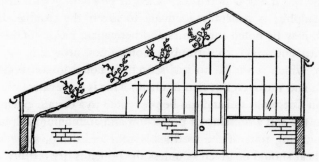

Training a vine in a vinery

Summer pruning and treatment

A vine has to be thinned by removal of shoots but this must be done gradually as removing too much foliage at one time can upset the balance of growth. The vine is of course nourished by its leaf so a certain amount of discretion has to be exercised. Greenhouse vines are spur-pruned and a spur will generally carry two good buds. Shoots will arise not only from these plump buds but secondary and axillary buds will start to shoot. All such buds should be rubbed out as soon as they start to swell or if shoots have formed these should be removed. It is better to have two shoots only at a spur as too much foliage prevents light and air getting at the plant and this lack of air may lead to mildew.

Many books on vine growing advocate damping down but I have never found this necessary or desirable. Dry warmth has proved entirely successful, that is conditions which allow tomatoes to be grown in the same greenhouse as the vines. From the beginning of April two lights are kept open a few inches at the extreme ends of the greenhouse and, depending on the temperature, the door is often open all day while from the start of June the greenhouse door is only closed in wet cold weather. Sun heat will be quite sufficient from then onwards until September and, unless a particularly long spell of cold wet weather sets in, the vines will progress quite happily with a minimum of attention. Provided the air has remained dry there is little likelihood of mildew but if any is noted then a slight powdering with dispersible sulphur is generally adequate to arrest the trouble. Leaf scorch may be noted sometimes and here again moist conditions seem to encourage this trouble. Sometimes browning of the leaves, which is similar to leaf scorch, is noted in soil poor in potash and nitrogen but rich in chalk. This is a prevalent condition on Cotswold soil and can be prevented to a certain extent by giving the soil a dressing of potassium and ammonium sulphate. At flowering time, if the weather is cold and damp, some artificial heat should be given as unless the pollen is dry fertility will be low. To cause fertilization the vines are tapped smartly with a cane or a hand can be passed gently over the bunches. The latter procedure often results in too many grapelets becoming fertilized which will later have to be pruned away, so I have not used this method recently, with the result that less berries have developed on the bunch and this has facilitated thinning out. The exception to this is Muscat of Alexandria which is a shy setter and has to be fertilized. The bunches of greenhouse grapes are normally thinned out by cutting away about one third of the grapelets when they are smaller than peas and before they start to get crowded. This must always be done for dessert grapes but is not always essential when the grapes are to be used for wine except in those varieties which naturally grow tight bunches. In these cases as the individual grapes swell the pressure causes many to burst, with the result that the whole becomes mouldy. (See plates 28 and 29.)

Feeding the vine

As the vine is prolific in growth it requires feeding; but this should be done with discretion. Feeding is unnecessary and undesirable when vines are young but they can be planted into compost to encourage good root growth; manures of any kind should be avoided. After the vine has reached the age for cropping there are two stages at which feeding is desirable. Between the period of the setting of the fruit and ripening cautious treatment with dried blood or a balanced artificial manure can be helpful while in the winter months a good top dressing is important. For this purpose it is usual to use an organic manure one year and follow the next two years with inorganic fertilizers. Pig manure is very suitable as it is high in potash but any manure will serve; dried blood is frequently used in greenhouses. For inorganic dressings some attention must be paid to the nature of the soil. If it is loamy then some chalk is required while if the soil is calcareous then an excess of potassium and ammonium sulphate are needed. A good balanced fertilizer which can be used both inside and outside the greenhouse is made of one part of potassium sulphate, one part of ammonium sulphate and two parts of basic slag. After the grapes have been picked the vine should be given as much air as possible and the house be allowed to go cold. When the leaves have dropped winter pruning should take place. This consists in cutting off all the laterals to a thick bud near the main stem and shortening the new vine or any extension growth on the old vine by about one third. After pruning the vine should be cleaned. Loose bark can be pulled off but scraping is neither desirable nor necessary. The cane should then be painted with lime sulphur to which a little tar winter wash oil has been added. The next step is to untie the canes and bend them down, tying or pegging the ends as low as possible till the new shoots have started to grow.

GREENHOUSE GRAPES FOR WINE MAKING

If it is decided to grow grapes for wine making in a greenhouse the choice is wide as many outdoor grapes such as the Muscadine are suitable for growing under glass. The Muscadine, also called Chasselas or Fendant, is an early water grape while another water grape which is early and suitable for wine is Foster's Seedling. Black Alicante is undoubtedly the most suitable greenhouse grape for red wine making as the skins are dark, the berries not too large and the juice has a suitable acidity. The bunches of Black Alicante are large and if the berries are thinned out then they also become quite large but for wine making this pruning is undesirable. Another red grape suitable for wine making and a favourite for greenhouse cultivation is Black Hamburgh, partly because it is vigorous in growth and matures early and also because the bunches are fairly open and do not require much thinning. Unlike normal outdoor wine grapes the proportion of skin to juice in greenhouse grapes is much less. Therefore to ensure a good red wine it is desirable to press the grapes and remove half their juice, converting this into a white wine, and then fermenting the remaining juice with the skins into a red wine.

There are not many muscat flavoured grapes which ripen early and are juicy enough for wine making but Rivers' Cotehouse Seedling is a finely-flavoured juicy muscat grape which ripens

early enough not to require external heat. It is of course possible
to ripen grapes, or anyhow many varities of grapes, without
external heat but even in a cold house it is desirable to apply a
little heat overnight during the month of March. This will enable the vines to get away to a good start and ensure ripening
during the early autumn while the weather is still dry. When ripe
grapes are exposed to moist conditions they tend to go mouldy
and it is quite possible to make a real Sauterne from greenhouse
grapes by allowing them to grow the 'noble' mould after ripening. This will reduce the acid content of the juice and increase the
sugar content, but such ennobling is only suitable for white
grapes. Red grapes which have gone mouldy must not be used for
making red wine as the mould destroys the colour and causes
bitterness.

It may interest the reader to compare the sugar concentration,
gravity and acid content of different greenhouse grapes. I am

TABLE XIV

GRAVITY, SUGAR AND ACID CONTENT OF ENGLISH GREEN-
HOUSE GRAPES COMPARED WITH IMPORTED GREEK
MUSCADINE GRAPES

	Gravity	% Sugar	% Acid as Citric
Greek Grapes 1953	82	19·4	0·65
Greek Grapes 1954	78	18·0	0·7
Appley Towers	84	20·0	1·20
Black Alicante	(68	16·6	1·54*
	(80	24·0	0·95*
Black Hamburgh	80	19·0	0·75*
Boowood Muscat	88	21·2	0·94
Buckland Sweetwater	73	16·4	0·77
Cotehouse Seedling	74	18·0	0·98*
„ Mouldy	97	24·0	0·80*
Foster's Seedling	70	17	0·70*
Golden Queen	85	20·2	0·87
Gros Colmar	65	14·4	0·75*
Gros Maroc	76	18·0	0·95
Lady Downe's	81	18·8	1·20
Lady Hutt	75	20·6	0·81
Madresfield Court	100	24·0	0·70
Muscat of Alexandria	87	22·0	0·77*
Mrs. Pinces Black Muscat	100	23·4	0·80

indebted to Messrs. Thomas Rivers and Son Ltd., of Sawbridge-worth, Herts, who specialize in the commercial cultivation of greenhouse grapes, for the supply of a range of grapes ripened in their greenhouses. Others grown in Almondsbury are also included, these being marked with an asterisk.

GRAPE VARIETIES FOR GREENHOUSE GROWING

Obtainable from: Messrs Th. Rivers and Son Ltd., Sawbridge-worth, Herts. (See plate 30.)

Appley Towers

This is a non-muscat grape of excellent flavour and dark colour, the berry somewhat elongated and bunches large and well formed. This grape keeps well.

Black Alicante, also called Black Tokay

Is recommended for heated houses but will mature sufficiently for wine making in a cold house. Large bunches, non-muscat flavour, somewhat acid in cold house, berries large and oval. The fruit is red and the skin very dark.

Black Hamburgh

Is a very well-known grape, the bunches of which are medium sized and the berries round and juicy and non-muscat in flavour. Black Hamburgh has an open growth, so requires less thinning out than other varieties. Will grow well in a cold house and in sheltered positions outdoors.

Black Muscat, also called Muscat Hamburgh

A very highly-flavoured muscat grape, of open growth. Suitable for both cold and warm houses.

Bowood Muscat

This green muscat-flavoured grape is very similar to Muscat of Alexandria in shape and flavour though the berries are rather less fleshy and therefore more juicy; here again the acidity is low, the sugar content high and the juice contains a good bit of pectin which gives it an attractive richness. Only suitable for heated houses.

Buckland Sweetwater

This non-muscat grape is low in acid, very juicy and sweet, berries are pale amber, round and large. The vines are vigorous and great bearers; will grow in cold houses.

Canon Hall Muscat

Requires heat and is late. Bunches and berries are large and round.

Cotehouse Seedling

Large bunches, round and amber, muscat flavoured and early. Good bearer, will mature in a cold house, though slowly.

Esperione

Is a great bearer, berries are large, round and black. Will ripen in a cold house.

Foster's Seedling

This grape is particularly suitable for wine making. If picked while still green it has a suitable acidity and gravity for light dry wines. When the skins have yellowed a little, a more fully bodied wine results. The berries are thin skinned and must be well thinned, as otherwise they tend to split. Dry conditions are desirable during maturing.

Golden Queen

Is a late grape, non-acid, very sweet and somewhat fleshy. Will mature rather late in a cold house.

Gros Colmar

A favourite hothouse grape and much cultivated abroad. The bunches are large but the fruit is often somewhat immature and remains green at the base. The juice is not very sweet but has a rather characteristic flavour. Best flavour results if grown in a heated house.

Gros Maroc

The bunches of Gros Maroc are large and round while the individual berries are huge, somewhat oval in shape and juicy, of a becoming acidity and non-muscat in flavour.

Lady Downe's

Bunches are long, berries large, black and somewhat fleshy. Requires heat, is well-flavoured, non-muscat.

Lady Hutt

This is another grape requiring heat. White, not very large, late but good keeper.

Madresfield Court

Is one of the finest black muscat grapes. It is early, very sweet and juicy, thin skinned and bunches are elongated. Will mature in a cold house.

Mrs. Pince's Black Muscat

These grapes grow in long bunches. Late but sweet and non-acid with small reddish black berries. This grape is the most suitable for the production of port wine. Requires some heat.

Muscat of Alexandria

Undoubtedly the most famous of muscat grapes, the berries are green, fleshy and oval in shape in bunches which are somwhat narrow and elongated. This grape will only develop a good muscat flavour when fully ripe when it will have a high sugar content, ranging between 20–22 per cent, and a low acid content. It is a shy setter and must be encouraged by tapping the canes in a dry atmosphere. Only develops well in heat.

GRAPE VARIETIES FOR OUTDOOR PLANTING

There are many grape varities suitable for growing outdoors and many are being tested for their suitability in various parts of Southern England. On the whole the Hybrid varieties are to be preferred as they ripen early and are less trouble to look after, being less prone to mildew. It is held that the wine made from Hybrid varieties is not so fine in flavour as wine from European grapes but when the choice lies between a fully ripe hybrid grape and a non-ripe or barely-ripe European grape then the former will yield a better wine without any shadow of doubt. There are of course some early-ripening European varieties such as the Sylvaner and the Sylvaner Riesling. Unlike the French Hybrids, obtained by crossing the American Vitis Rupestris with European vines, Sylvaner Riesling is crossbred from two European vines. Such vines are not normally spoken of as Hybrids but are frequently called by the names of the vines used for crossing. It may be of interest to discuss here how a new variety is produced. Briefly the vines are cross-fertilized as follows: before the flowers open the cap which encloses the stamens is pulled off and the male stamens are removed to prevent natural fertilization. A paper bag is then tied over the flower to protect it from accidental fertilization and at blossoming time the stamens from the vine which is to be used for crossing are dusted on to the female pistil of the castrated vine. Generally the late varieties are used as the female plant, as they yield more satisfactory seedlings. The mature grapes are removed in the autumn and the seeds are sown. These cross-bred seedlings have then to be tested and very few come up to expectation. Seedling 88, a more recent crossing of the Riesling and the Sylvaner, known as the Scheurebe, is different in character from the well known Sylvaner Riesling and has the following advantages over its parents (see plate 31). It is luxuriant, is lime resistant when grafted on American Stock 5 BB, has a stronger bouquet than Riesling and ripens about two weeks earlier with a gravity higher by 10 to 15 degrees. It is resistant to frost and chlorosis and thrives on poor soil. It is reputed to yield a wine of superlative character. This vine grafted on Teleki 5 BB is growing vigorously and cropping well in the author's vineyard. It is being tested for its quality when grown as an ungrafted variety and such plants will be for sale in a few years time. Scheurebe is a recent vine but there are many well-known and successful vine varieties of which the following is a recommended selection. As indicated previously the fact that they have proved profitable either abroad or in this country is no guarantee that they will be equally productive in every vineyard or on every soil in which they may be planted.

EUROPEAN VINES FOR WHITE WINE

Sylvaner	Muscadine (also called Chasselas,
Madeleine Royal	Fendant, Gutedel)
Sylvaner Riesling	Scheurebe
Riesling	

EUROPEAN VINES FOR RED WINE

Gamay	Red Muscadine
Blue Portuguese	Early Burgundy
Late Burgundy	Chablis Haut Noir (a Pinot)

Black Hamburgh (Good on chalk, requires sheltered position)

Hybrid Vines for White Wine

Seyve Villard 5/276	Chenin Blanc
Seibel 5279	Excelsior
Seibel 5409	

Hybrid Vines for Red Wine

Seibel 5455	Seibel 2010
Seibel 13053	Seyve Villard 5/247
Triumph of Alsace	

Triumph of Alsace is early ripening and high in sugar content.

Grape varieties tested in the Almondsbury Vineyard

A selection of vines were grown in the author's vineyard but only a few have proved their worth so far. Some vines take rather longer to establish themselves and may therefore become more productive with increase in age. From the experience gained so far the following have been chosen as the most successful for laying down a vineyard.

Vines for White Wine Production

Seyve Villard 5/276	Sylvaner
Sylvaner Riesling	Excelsior
Chenin Blanc	Scheurebe
Riesling	Chasselas

Vines for Red Wine Production

Seibel 5455	Blue Portuguese
Chablis Haut Noir	Triumph of Alsace
Seibel 13053	Baco No. 1

OTHER VARIETIES OF VINES BEING GROWN
(Some are still under test.)

White Grapes

Pearl of Czaba   Tokay Frontignan
Cotehouse Seedling   Madeleine Royal
Ascot Citronelle

Two other Hybrid varieties, both white, which are reputed to be prolific are:

Seibel 5279   Seibel 5409

Red Grapes

Early Burgundy   Late Burgundy
  (These will probably be acceptable but are slow to produce their fruit.)

Chasselas rose   Blue Silk
Brant   Seyve Villard 5/247
Black Hamburgh

TABLE XV

SUGAR AND ACID CONTENT OF GRAPES GROWN IN ENGLISH VINEYARDS

Data recorded by Tritton (Almondsbury Vineyard)

	% Sugar			% Acid as Citric	
	Oct. 3	Oct. 17	Nov. 29	Oct. 3	Nov. 29
Seibel 13053	14	17	—	1·85	—
Gamay	12	—	—	2·29	—
Baco No. 1	10	—	—	2·4	—
Madeleine Ambree	12	—	—	1·7	—
Seyve Villard 5-276	13	17	—	1·4	—
Seibel 5279	12·2	—	—	1·44	—
Chenin Blanc	11·8	17	—	1·30	—
Seibel 5455	12·2	18	—	—	—
Blue Portuguese	12·4	17	18·6	1·65	0·9
Tokay Frontignan	20·4	—	23·4	1·54	—
Excelsior	—	18	—	—	—
Scheurebe (2 year old)	12	14	—	—	—
Riesling (5 year old)	12·3	14·5	—	—	—

Data recorded by Brock (Surrey Vineyard)

	12% Sugar on	15% Sugar on	17% Sugar on
Madeleine Royal	Aug. 3	Sept. 3	Oct. 11
Gamay	Sept. 7	Sept. 22	—
Muscat Hamburgh	Sept. 8	Oct. 16	—
Chasselas	Sept. 15	Oct. 16	—
White Frontignan	Sept 25	Oct. 30	—
Blue Portuguese	Sept. 24	Oct. 20	—
Riesling	Sept. 30	Oct. 30	—

DATA FROM GERMAN VINEYARDS

Vintage 1952	Sugar Content of Grapes		
	Sept. 23	Oct. 8	Oct. 20
Elbling and Räuschling	13·5%	18·5%	—
Müller Thürgau	18%	22·5%	—
Sylvaner	16%	21%	—
Riesling	18%	25%	—
Chasselas	—	—	17%
Late Burgundy	—	—	21–29%

Vintage 1953	Sugar Content of Grapes				
	Sept. 1	Sept. 16	Oct. 1	Oct. 5	Oct. 16
Müller Thürgau	15·6%	20%	22%	—	—
Sylvaner	13%	17·5%	19·6%	—	20·5%
Riesling	12·5%	17·8%	20%	—	22%
Blue Portuguese	—	—	—	16–20%	—
Müller Thürgau	—	—	—	16–31%	—

	Gravities recorded in (1953) bracketed and 1954			
	Sept. 1	Sept. 16	Oct. 1	Oct. 10
Müller Thürgau	(71) 37	(88) 59	(94) 64	—
Sylvaner	(61) 29	(78) 48	(85) 59	(89) 67
Riesling	(58) 22	(79) 38	(86) 56	(93) 69

These figures show that German gravities and sugar contents
do not differ appreciably from recorded British figures. It must be
remembered that the data from English vineyards refers to young
vines. These produce smaller bunches which ripen later than those
on older vines and there is no reason therefore why, when such
vines have matured, better gravities should not result than those
recorded in Table XV. By selective gathering of berries musts of

higher gravities can be obtained even in poor years as individual berries vary in their sugar content.

The Purchase of Vines, Sources of Supply and Licences

Most of the vines listed above, both indoor and outdoor varieties, are now obtainable from various sources in Britain. Messrs Thomas Rivers and Sons Ltd., Sawbridgeworth, Herts., specialize in indoor vines while Horticultural Utilities, Formby, Lancs, grow outdoor varieties for sale. Some hybrid vines are obtainable from the Almondsbury Vineyard. Many vines can also be purchased from Germany, France and Switzerland and the names of some foreign suppliers are:

Germany: Paul Müller,
                  Eltville am Rhein,
                      Western Germany,

France: Vilmorin Andrieux,
                  4 Quai de la Mégisserie,
                      Paris, France.

Switzerland: Jacob Kaltbrunner,
                  Erlenbach, Zürich,
                  Switzerland.

Anyone wishing to import vines from abroad has to apply to the Board of Trade for an Import Licence, stating the value of the vines including cost of transport so as to secure the necessary currency. Air transport is desirable so as to avoid delays. Imported vines have to be accompanied by a health certificate issued by the Ministry of Agriculture of the country of origin and they are again inspected on arrival in this country by an Agricultural Officer. Plants should not be dispatched till an import licence has been received and as the issuing of licences takes time those wishing to acquire vines from abroad are well advised to make their plans in good time.

VINE PROPAGATION, PLANTING AND TRAINING

Vine Propagation

There are various methods of propagating vines but they all consist of taking either buds or pieces of bud-bearing wood and striking them in soil. Vines are not normally grown from seeds as the seedlings frequently do not come true, hence only vegetative reproduction is practised. Vines can be propagated from a single bud which is pegged down on to a piece of turf about six inches square and three inches deep. First the turves are treated with boiling water poured on to the grassy side to kill both grass and insects, they are then put grass side down on to slates and left to dry. When nearly dry a piece is scooped out from the centre of the turf and some sand and charcoal is put in its place. The eye, which is cut out with a sharp knife by scooping underneath the bud taking about half the depth of the cane with it, is pressed into the sand and charcoal mixture with the bud uppermost and is lightly covered with soil. The whole is then kept moist when root growth will soon be noted. As soon as the roots have filled the turf it can be planted in a pot or box using a mixture of peat, sand and good loam. Alternatively eyes with some adherent wood can be also struck by planting directly into a small pot or several eyes are planted into a larger pot. If a slanting cut is made behind the bud the slanted side can be brought close to the wall of the pot which will assist in root formation. The soil, which should be light and friable, is kept warm and the pot stood in a moist atmosphere while the bud must remain covered by soil. The value of growing a vine from a single bud is that a very good root system is set up and by the time this young plant is strong enough to produce a shoot the ball of root will have become quite considerable. Such a plant can be transplanted into its permanent quarters when a year old and will often yield fruit at three years.

Vines can also be propagated from cane prunings. Preferably these should be no more than ten inches long and should carry about three buds but some growers strike cuttings as long as twelve inches in which case they carry from four to five buds. The wood should be short or medium noded and it is very important that all of the cuttings are free from axillary growth. Root production at the nodes is very much less vigorous when the buds are thin and pointed instead of plump and well-nourished. Before planting or at pruning time the wood is cut straight across immediately below a bud and at an angle of about 45° about one inch above the topmost bud. By being cut at a slant less water is likely to seep into the wood and therefore the wood is less likely to frost damage. The prunings can be planted at once provided that the soil is damp and likely to remain so or they can be bundled up and stored in damp sand till the early spring when they are planted out. Generally they are inserted in an upright position into a deep hole with the topmost bud a few inches above the soil, which should be made quite firm round the cutting, and some soft friable soil should be heaped over the bud to prevent it from drying out. If cuttings are planted in compost or good soil they may produce a shoot anything from three to five feet high by the end of the summer, but despite this the root structure will be rather poor. It is not advisable to transplant these cuttings till they are two years old, that is they should have a further year in the nursery bed. If it is decided nevertheless to use these one-year-old plants for vineyard stock then they should not be lifted till May when they are transferred to their permanent quarters. Copious watering of the soil is required till such time as the plant is well established.

Planting the vine

Whether the new plant has been grown from a cutting or from a bud it must be well planted, that is a very considerable hole must be made in the ground which is filled with compost. The roots should first be dipped into 5 per cent solution of tar oil as this disinfection seems to stimulate root growth and then they should all be shortened by about a third. This will encourage further growth of fine rootlets. The plant is inserted into the hole and covered with compost which should be watered in to assist it to consolidate around the root. Sifted compost is preferable to rough compost and a small addition of lime is advisable. The top bud should be about soil level or just obtruding and when the soil has been made firm some earth is heaped over it to prevent the bud from drying out. If the vine is to be planted against a wall or a house then a plant grown from a cane should be inserted at an angle with the roots as far away from the house as possible. If a pot plant is used it is again desirable to place it some distance from the house and to train the shoot on a cane towards the wall, protecting it from accidental breakage by surrounding it with wire netting.

Vineyard Planting and Management

It depends very much on the lie of the land how a vineyard should be laid out and how the vines should be trained. If the vines are planted on a steep slope then training on individual stakes will facilitate the cultivation of the ground and summer pruning. Such a method is adopted very extensively on the steep slopes of the vineyards situated in the valleys of the Mosel and the Rhine and on many hillsides in Switzerland. If vines are planted on level ground then it is very usual not to stake the individual plants but to train the shoots on wires. Sometimes vines are not staked at all but the shoots, when they start to set their fruit and the bunches become heavy, are supported on forked tree branches. Stakes, especially in this country, are very much more expensive than canes so a compromise can be reached by training the young vine on a cane and then as the vine becomes older wiring this cane to wires stretched between two strong wooden or metal posts. Planting distances can vary considerably but between one and one and a quarter yards is a suitable distance to have both between the plants and between the rows. On the other hand, where space is no object the rows are better planted further apart, which allows for ease in cultivation and will eventually lead to greater productivity as more sun can get at the plants. Rows, wherever possible, should be planted from north to south while the aspect of hills should be south or south-east. It is quite easy to ascertain the best direction for the rows by setting a stake and taking the direction of the shadow at noon as a guiding line.

Spring planting is preferable as root growth is more vigorous in warm soil and the plant becomes established more quickly. The methods advocated earlier of disinfecting the roots, shortening them by a third and planting them into compost to which a little lime has been added should be followed. If the plants have been in transit they should be soaked in water for a few hours before cutting back their roots.

Either one- or two-year-old plants should be acquired as young plants are easier to establish than older ones. These plants may arrive already pruned or if grown in the owner's vineyard should be pruned back to two buds early in February. As soon as the buds begin to shoot the one which appears to shoot less vigorously should be rubbed out; this can be done by moving the soil away from the cane by hand and inspecting the strength of the shoot. The soil is again heaped round the stump to prevent the budding shoot from drying out. As it emerges from the soil the shoot is tied to a stake. Any axillary growth which is noted must of course be pinched out. In February of the following year it is cut back to the desired height which may range, according to the type of training that is chosen, from twelve to thirty inches off the ground. All the lower buds are removed and the two topmost buds are allowed to develop into shoots which are tied to a cane. Although flowers may form on these shoots they should not be allowed to grow and all axillary growth must be removed if formed. At the end of August the shoots are cut back to about five feet or even less depending upon the vigour of growth. Both of them should be pencil thick as no fruit may be expected in the following year if the canes are less than pencil thick and unless they have hardened thoroughly. At pruning time, which can be between December and the end of February, the canes are cut back according to the method of training to be adopted. If, for instance, Goblet pruning is decided upon then the stem should be about twelve inches high and carry two shoots, each of which will be cut back to two buds. If it is desired to adopt Head pruning then both shoots which have arisen on the stem will have hardened to canes and the upper cane and part of the stem are cut right off immediately above the lower cane. The latter is shortened to one good eye and several secondary eyes all of which should form shoots. Four shoots are retained which in the following year are cut back to one good eye. For Guyot pruning the stronger cane is cut back to six buds and the other to two, while if the vines are to be Cordon trained both canes will be retained and cut back as required. These various methods of training are discussed under separate headings and frankly all of them seem to be satisfactory, as in every case the growth is restricted. Any ripe wood that is cut away can be used for propagation purposes.

When the vines have been pruned and the vineyard cleaned up then it is time to top dress the soil. It is usual to give a dressing of farmyard manure in one year (usually in the autumn) and inorganic fertilizers for the two successive years (usually after pruning). The same mixture of inorganic fertilizers as used for greenhouse vines can be used, namely one part ammonium sulphate, one part potassium sulphate and two parts basic slag, but these proportions or the ingredients can be varied to suit the circumstances.

Spring work in the vineyard

Vines tend to produce basal shoots which are called water sprouts. They must always be removed and will pull or break off quite easily. The stem should also be kept free of growth, any shoots emerging being at once rubbed off. Before the rise of sap in the plant any long canes should either be pegged down to the ground or bent in such a way that the buds nearest to the stem are at the highest point and the end buds at a lower point on the cane. This encourages the buds to break close to the stem. Failing this the biggest shoots will be at the tip of the cane and consequently the most fruitful buds will have to be cut off in the following year, unless the entire length of the cane is spur pruned. During the spring wires have to be tightened, the vines tied in and the ground kept clean while any axillary growth must be pinched out as soon as noted. All shoots must be secured to prevent damage from wind by either tying to a wire or tucking between a double row of wires.

Summer work in the vineyard

During the late spring and early summer vines should receive several sprayings with colloidal copper or Bordeaux mixture. Starting from the time the leaves have opened till about the middle of August four applications of copper are required and this should be followed at two fortnightly intervals with sulphur dusting or spraying. If the weather is dry or the vines grown in an open position less spraying is required than where the vines grow in sheltered humid conditions and in any garden where roses suffer from American Blight spraying is strongly advocated. Boot's Colloidal Copper called Buisol and their Colloidal Sulphur Sulsol are easy to handle and effective but any preparation of copper and sulphur will serve.

Copper is used to prevent a mould called Peronospora (*Plasmopara viticola*), while sulphur prevents the occurrence of Oidium or Downy Mildew (*Uncinula necator*). During the summer the vines must be kept from growing too much leaf and this is done by pinching out axillary growth and shortening fruiting shoots beyond the flower. Some flowers should be removed from overvigorous vines such as Seyve Villard 5/276 as otherwise they will overcrop and suffer a setback for several years. At the end of August tall replacement shoots can be shortened a little and loose shoots be tied to stakes. By this time the shoots should be pencil thick and only if they are of that size will they be fruitful. The most pleasant part of summer work is undoubtedly the harvesting of the grapes. In some localities vines, especially red ones, have to be netted to prevent the birds from devouring the lot. In France the bird population is kept severely restricted and consequently the vines do not require such protection. Apart from bird scarers, which are usually of doubtful value, there is no alternative to netting or draping with butter muslin. Grapes should be harvested as ripe as possible. Sometimes it pays to leave the grapes on the vine till after leaf fall as varieties like the Riesling, which mature late, hang well (see plate 32). The later the grape is harvested the more sugar it will contain. This is shown in Table XV where the increase of sugar due to ripening is recorded. When harvesting the grapes these should be cut and not pulled off as that will damage the vine. Any mouldy grapes are preferably cut away. Throughout the summer it is desirable to keep the soil clean and aerated as cultivating the ground will assist the vines to ripen.

Winter work in the vineyard

When the leaves have fallen they should be dug in or raked off and burned. The soil can then receive a mulch of manure which is left till the vines are to be pruned when organic manure is turned in. On calcareous soil better results are obtained by giving each year a dressing of two parts potassium sulphate, one part ammonium sulphate and one part basic slag. Superphosphate should not be used on soils with high lime content. Heavy soils are best kept open and light by digging in cinders or covering with ashes. Soils poor in humus benefit by hop manure and sandy soils require farmyard manure above all else. No general directions can be given as they cannot always apply on account of the many variations in soil which exist, but textbooks on vineyard management generally advocate farmyard manure after the first crop, and inorganic manures containing potassium, nitrogen and phosphorous during the following two years. The grower who understands his soil will soon appreciate how best to treat his vines, particularly as deficiencies will soon show up in leaf colour and act as a guide to future treatment of the soil. From December onward the vines can be pruned (see pruning section later). The earlier they are pruned the sooner they will shoot but in this country outdoor pruning can be undertaken till the end of

February. Generally late pruning is advocated as then the wood will have had more time to ripen. Although the vine will shoot later there is the advantage that the young growth will not be exposed to late frosts.

Vines on Pergolas and House Walls

There is very little that need be said here which has not already been mentioned under training. Most people who plant vines against walls wish to know the quickest way to cover a wall and to obtain fruit at the same time. Naturally a vigorous grower like Black Hamburgh will cover the space earlier than a slower grower such as a Muscadine. Provided the aspect is south and sheltered, Black Hamburgh is ideal. Even then one can hardly expect one vine to cover a wall in a year or so and for quick results I would advise training two or three vines at different heights, using the single and double cordon. The vines should be attached to wires which are fastened to metal bars six inches away from the wall as otherwise mildew is likely.

Vine training and yield of fruit

The Guyot method of training a vine is probably that most extensively used on the Continent but growers in France whose vineyards are on poor calcareous soil have informed me that on such soils the method did not prove productive, but that head or goblet pruning gave better yields. On Cotswold soil similar results were noted, the vines which were head pruned producing larger leaves and better bunches. However, definite conclusions cannot be drawn unless comparisons have been made over a number of years. In parts of Germany, particularly in the Mosel Valley, the vine growers claim that they obtain better yields because of the particular methods of training they have adopted. Following their methods might not necessarily produce the same results in other parts of Germany or in countries with slightly cooler climates and here again the vine grower will have to

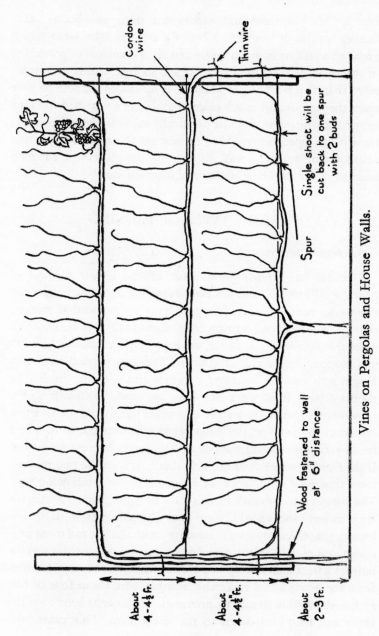

Cordon wire

Thin wire

Single shoot will be
cut back to one spur
with 2 buds

Spur

Wood fastened to wall
at 6" distance

About 4-4½ ft.

About 4-4½ ft.

About 2-3 ft.

Vines on Pergolas and House Walls.

exercise his judgment and experiment until he obtains satisfactory results. It is always a bit of a mystery why vines which grow up a wall or in greenhouses can yield hundreds of pounds of of grapes while vines in vineyards yield so little, hardly ever much more than five pounds per plant. It is no doubt because to save space they are usually much closer together in a vineyard and they have to be pruned much more drastically to get both the wood and the fruit to ripen because they do not get the reflected heat that assists a vine against a wall. By keeping the plants low a certain amount of reflected heat is obtained from the soil.

VARIOUS TYPES OF PRUNING

Guyot pruning and training

Mention has already been made of the Guyot method of pruning. When the stem has been cut to the desirable height, say twenty to twenty-four inches, two buds are retained at pruning time. The two shoots arising from these buds will be tied to a stake throughout the summer, are kept free from axillary growth and stopped at the end of August. They are pruned back to a longer arm with six buds and a shorter arm with two buds. The shoots arising from these two buds are treated similarly to the previous year, tying to a stake etc, while the shoots which grow out from the buds on the longer cane will bear the fruit. These fruit bearing shoots are stopped at three leaves beyond the flower. If the fruiting shoot does not bear that year then the two replacement shoots are not likely to be very fruitful in the following year. The longer cane should in this case be spur pruned while the replacement canes should be cut back to one bud each. In the following year these shoots will produce much thicker and more productive canes. The fruiting cane should always be bent down to the bottom wire which should be between eighteen and twenty inches from the ground and preferably another wire about four or five inches above this should be provided. The cane is bent over the latter and then tied down to the lower wire. This causes the cane to have its highest point near the trunk and the downward slope will ensure that the shoots will break evenly rather than having the largest shoots at the end. At each node of the fruiting cane young shoots will emerge which can be held in place by passing them between a double wire fixed about eighteen inches above the lowest wire. If only a single wire is provided the shoots have to be tied to this.

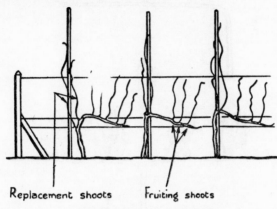

Replacement shoots   Fruiting shoots

Guyot pruning and training

Cordon training and Spur pruning

Vines can be trained on walls or on wires as a single or double cordon. The single cordon is produced by a single shoot arising from a stem, this shoot being trained out sideways to form a cordon. For a double cordon the young vine is cut back to two buds at the required height. These are allowed to shoot and all other buds are rubbed out; these shoots are pulled down to a horizontal wire and tied. At pruning time each cane is cut back to a well-ripened portion, probably by about one-third. In the following year shoots will arise from buds all along these canes, now called cordons and will grow up vertically. The end shoot is trained out horizontally till the cordon has attained the desired length. Each of these vertical shoots is pruned back to a short spur carrying two buds hence the term spur pruning. In the following spring two shoots will grow from each spur and in due course each is cut back to only one bud so that the cordon is furnished with two spurs at each node. To cover a wall quickly

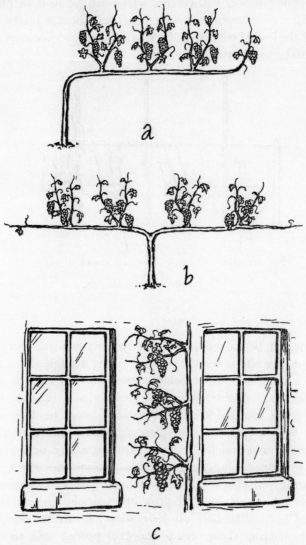

(*a*) Single cordon, (*b*) Double cordon, (*c*) Upright cordon between windows a double cordon can be used for the lower portion of the wall and a single cordon trained over the double cordon, say about a yard above it.

Head pruning

This involves the forming of a head as is done in the growing of gooseberries. The first year's shoot is cut back to two buds with the lower bud at the required height to form a stem. In the following year two shoots will grow from the top two buds. Any others which may arise are rubbed out. The shoots are tied on to a stake and at pruning time the top shoot and the stem are cut back to the bottom shoot. This is cut back to one bud and from this bud and some secondary buds shoots will grow. Four of these are retained and tied out fanwise or left unsupported. These shoots, which will have hardened to canes, are again cut back to one bud at pruning time.

Goblet pruning

Alternatively the trunk, which should be about twelve inches high, may be trained into a Goblet shape by letting two to four shoots mature and cutting them back at pruning time to a couple of good stout buds. Several straight arms will develop in Goblet shape.

Various additional methods of training vines

Some methods of pruning and training which are practised in Germany may prove of interest. The young canes may be shortened to say ten or twelve buds, then bent into a circle and tied down to the trunk. Alternatively, if they emerge from a Goblet shape or branched trunk, they may be tied to several stakes surrounding the vine.

A third method is used extensively in the valley of the Mosel and is considered to be particularly productive. The growers there claim that the yield per plant is about 30 per cent more than the average and consider that this is due to allowing longer and more shoots to develop and to keeping more leaf on the plant. In this method four canes at four different heights on a permanent stem are retained, bent into a circle and tied to the stake supporting the permanent stem (see figure 3 below).

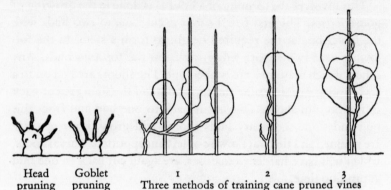

Head   Goblet   I   2   3
pruning   pruning   Three methods of training cane pruned vines

DEFICIENCY DISEASES OF VINES

It has often been said that vines bear better the poorer the soil but this generalization is not strictly in accordance with the experience of vineyard owners. What is true is that anything which produces sappy growth like excess nitrogen or manure on rich soils will inevitably lead to unripe wood and hence to lack of fruiting buds. Therefore if a young vine is planted into fertile soil no manuring will be required for a year or so but after cropping the essential elements must be replaced. If this is not done then the vine will show deficiencies by alteration in leaf colour and other troubles. Conversely, a vine will grow equally well on stoney or slatey soil provided it is regularly nourished.

Vines need potassium, phosphorus and nitrogen, some lime and magnesium, boron and manganese in traces and iron which is always present in soils. Of all these undoubtedly potassium is the most important as it helps the ripening of wood and fruit. If the soil is too acid then this must be corrected by the addition of lime and if it is too chalky then, unless the vines are grafted on a chalk-resistant root stock, additions must be made which will render the soil less alkaline. The most suitable addition for this purpose is ammonium sulphate, and as chalky soils are frequently low in nitrogen the addition of such an artificial nitrogen compound is also necessary. It might be thought that organic manure would be preferable but digging in farmyard manure often leads to the liberation of more chalk during the decomposition of the manure and hence to further disturbance of the balance of nutrients in the soil.

One of the most obvious signs of deficiency diseases in plants is chlorosis or the intense yellowing of foliage. Chlorosis in vines occurs if the plants are in stagnant sour soil, when in addition the shoots will develop black spots near the nodes. This yellowing will be followed by the leaves turning brown and finally red at the edges after which they will start to die off. Where chlorosis is due to excess of lime the yellowing is more intense and growth will become weak. In the latter case liberal applications of ammonium sulphate and some potash are indicated.

Lack of phosphorus also leads to poor growth and lack of fruitfulness, but leaves remain green unless the deficiency is severe when the leaf veins will become red in colour and brown spots appear on the margins of the leaves which will start to roll outwards and die off. Potassium is necessary to the vine and it helps to regulate the intake and output of moisture. Lack of this element is noticed by a violet discolouration of the upperside of the lower leaves followed by browning, after which the leaves die and fall off, the vine gradually becoming defoliated and un-productive. Magnesium deficiency is not very common, occurring mostly in acid light soil which may also be lacking in lime. Vines cannot grow without boron and leaves soon show lack of this by mosaic-like yellowing between the veins followed later by some rolling of the leaves. Lack of boron is again most noticeable on chalky soil. A dressing with basic slag will usually supply suffi-cient of any of the elements which are required in traces. Once the vine grower has learnt to recognize these danger signals he can soon adjust his soil to overcome them.

FUNGAL AND OTHER DISEASES OF VINES

Vines are liable to fungal diseases which can be prevented by regular application of copper and sulphur sprays. The grower will wish to know how to recognize the various diseases and the following notes may prove helpful:

Peronospora (Plasmopara viticola)

This is first noted as yellowish oily transparent patches (round on young leaves) turning later to white patches on the underside of the leaf.

Oidium tuckeri (Uncinula necator)

Soon after the vine has produced leaves some will appear wrinkled and both sides will be covered with a greyish dust. Berries will dry up or split and become unfit for wine making.

Leaf Scorch (Pseudopeziza tracheiphila)

This is also caused by a fungus but is less damaging than Peronospora or Oidium. This scorch shows up between the main veins of the leaf as brown patches in white grapes and as red patches in red grapes and is generally surrounded by a narrow yellow band in the former and a greenish yellow band in the latter. Vines which suffer from leaf scorch soon become bare and the yield of fruit is seriously affected. It is prevalent in hilly soils which lack humus. Copper spraying carried out as soon as the leaves unfold is effective.

Grey Mould (Botrytis cinerea)

Soft sappy growth is particularly prone to the ravages of this

226

fungus. In a greenhouse a buoyant atmosphere is one of the best preventatives while in moist humid conditions this fungus may easily effect grapes, causing rotting of stems and berries. When this mould attacks *ripe* grapes it can prove beneficial but in northern climates grapes are seldom ripe enough. This mould cannot be prevented by copper spraying but only by encouraging vigorous plant growth and allowing sufficient air to get at the vine and so allowing the grapes to dry quickly after rain.

Insect Pests

There are quite a few insects which attack grapes, but D.D.T. is generally effective.

Vines are frequently attacked by mites which cause the leaves to curl and become puckered. Prevention consists in spraying the dormant vines with 6 to 8 per cent tar winterwash oil or 1 to 2 per cent dinitro-orthocresol (D.N.C.). Red Spider can be removed by spraying with a D.D.T. or a phosphoric ester preparation.

Phylloxera

This is the name of the vine louse which affects both the leaves and roots of vines. The underside of the leaves become covered with galls while the roots develop nodules which soon render the whole root system useless, causing the plant to die. The vine louse has a complex life cycle and various types of phylloxera are known. Fortunately American vines are very resistant to phylloxera and much research is being carried out to evolve a chemical which will kill the louse in the soil and not prove harmful to the vine. Some measure of success has been attained but only time will tell how permanent the new remedies will prove.

7

The Vintner's Calendar
Work in the Vineyard and Winery

JANUARY

In the Vineyard

Prepare the soil for weathering by deep forking. Do not turn the sods but fork as deeply as possible. Apply equal parts of bone meal and a potassium fertilizer, and if needed some lime. If the soil is heavy dig in some peat. On warm days pruning may be started. Remove all leaves from soil and burn.

In the Winery

Keep all containers filled to the brim with the exception of sherry-type wines. Watch for secondary fermentation. Wine made from the earliest grapes must be kept very cold to induce clarification. Fruit wines and wines low in acid should be racked. Taste wines made from grapes; if not unduly acid, rack and use the yeast left behind to mix with the really sour grape wines. These should not be racked but the yeast deposit and additional yeast should be well mixed with the wine and racking delayed another month. Wines of previous years can be racked, avoiding contact with air as much as possible. Test wine for stability; it should not parken after eight hours exposure in a glass. If not stable, sulphite with one Campden tablet to the gallon.

FEBRUARY

In the Vineyard

Pruning should now start in earnest. The long bearing canes should have their tips pegged down to the soil to encouragethe young shoots to break evenly. Weak vines are cut back harder then strong ones such as the hybrids. Where there is evidence that certain vines do not crop well with Guyot pruning, change to head pruning by cutting back to main stem. One-year-old vines, if vigorous, should now be cut to the height which is desired for the permanent stem, anything from twelve to thirty inches. The lower shoots on these young plants are removed when there is no further fear of frost. The two top buds are allowed to develop into shoots to be trained as desired in subsequent years. In February all but one-year-old plants should be sprayed with dinitro-orthocresol (D.N.C.) or a mixture of this and tar winter wash oil. Brush the stems and the nodes from which shoots arise with Gishurst Compound or a sulphur suspension.

In the Winery

The second racking should now be carried out and aeration should be avoided as far as possible. Wines should be ready for blending. Older wines can be bottled, preferably on bright and fine days.

MARCH

In the Vineyard

Pruning should be finished by mid-March. Staking and fixing of wires should be attended to. On poor soils apply nitrogen containing artificial fertilizer in alternate years. Spray as in February but this type of spray should not be used after this month.

In the Winery

Second racking of acid wines should now be carried out.

Stable and clear wines can now be bottled. For the amateur the following test procedure is advocated. Transfer some racked clear wine to a bottle and bring this into a warm room. Cork. If no deposit of yeast is shown and pressure does not develop in the bottle during several weeks in the warm, the wine should be ready for bottling. Always bottle on fine days when the barometric pressure is high.

APRIL

In the Vineyard

Purchased vines are planted this month or in the month of March. Where leaf scorch occurred in previous years, two sprayings with Bordeaux mixture or colloidal copper must be carried out at a week's interval as soon as the buds swell.

In the Winery

Racking of acid wines should not be delayed beyond this month. Take note of the occurrence of secondary fermentation, remove bungs and insert fermentation traps. Bottle stable wines.

MAY

In the Vineyard

Tie in young shoots and spray with copper to combat Peronospora as soon as leaves are open. Either colloidal copper or Bordeaux mixture should be used but it must be rather weak. Repeat again in ten days time. If the weather is warm and sunny, sulphur should be applied as dust, if wet as a spray. This combats the mildew Oidium, but generally sulphur treatment can be deferred till June. Vines may be transplanted.

In the Winery

The wine should be allowed to rest this month. Keep barrels

full, watch for secondary fermentation and keep rooms or cellars well aired.

JUNE

In the Vineyard

If nitrogenous feeding is required apply some nitro-chalk or on chalky soil ammonium sulphate. No other manures should be used. During this month replacement shoots should be tied in. It is as well to remove tendrils which lead to tangling of foliage. Copper spraying is only required in humid atmospheres, otherwise continue with sulphur spraying or dusting only.

In the Winery

Wine should be allowed to rest and barrels kept full.

JULY

In the Vineyard

It is important to keep shoots tied in and laterals pinched out. Soil should be forked or hoed lightly, kept well aerated and free from weeds. Where soil is lacking in humus, green manuring or mulching with grass can be resorted to. Dust with sulphur. Copper spraying only required if weather is very humid. If caterpillars are noticed D.D.T. should be added to the sprays.

In the Winery

Prepare and sterilize containers and plant required for the vintage.

AUGUST

In the Vineyard

Hoe or fork the soil lightly. Cultivation, which keeps the soil open, aids in early ripening and is more important than manuring the vines. The tops of the replacement shoots may be pinched out as soon as browning at the nodes is noticed. Spray young vines.

In the Winery

Allow the wine to rest, keep winery well aired.

SEPTEMBER

In the Wineyard

Keep well weeded, prevent ravages from birds by netting red grapes, or if a few bunches are particularly cherished, cover them with paper bags. Wasp nests should be traced and eliminated. Wasps can be trapped in bottles of weak syrup. Spraying not needed.

In the Winery

Bottling should be carried out on stable wines, avoiding contact with air as much as possible. Filter hazy wines and yeast lees. New wines should receive their third racking at the end of the month. Do not sulphite unless absolutely necessary. Harvesting of early grapes may start this month. Red grapes should be carefully inspected and mouldy ones removed at the same time as the stalks. The mouldy grapes can be pressed for white wine but the resulting juice must be heavily sulphited.

OCTOBER

Harvest and start on the production of wine.

NOVEMBER

In the Vineyard

Rake up all leaves and burn. Manure with stable manure one year and in the following year with potassium containing fertilizer, basic slag and lime. (Nitrogen-containing fertilizers are better applied in the spring.) Young plants should not be manured, only vines which have cropped heavily.

In the Winery

Attend to the fermentation.

DECEMBER

In the Vineyard

Keep vineyard clean from fallen leaves and soil open. Burn all leaves.

In the Winery

Watch the fermentation and take wine off most of the lees when primary fermentation is finished. Transfer to clean casks.

Glossary of Terms used in Wine Making

ACETIFICATION: turning into acetic acid—vinegar being dilute acetic acid.

ACID: the sour constituent in wine which may be citric, tartaric, malic or lactic, but must not be acetic. The riper the grapes are the more tartaric and the less malic acid they contain. Malic acid is contained in many fruits but particularly in apples. When wine is allowed to stand on its yeast deposit during warm weather it frequently becomes less acid through the malic acid turning into a milder acid, namely lactic acid. This is the acid which is present in milk when it goes sour and this change to a milder acidity is known as the malo-lactic fermentation.

ALCOHOL: This when pure and rectified is a light-weight clear liquid produced by yeasts from sugar. An essential constituent of wines and spirits.

ANADA: a nursery for young sherry.

APERITIF: an appetizer wine.

BLENDING: mixing different varieties of a fruit before converting it into a juice such as a sour apple or grape with a sweet apple or grape. Also applied to mixing wines to adjust their flavour.

BODY: a wine which contains some extractive matter; the reverse of thin.

BOTTLES: for red table wines generally green bottles are used, for white table wines tall green or amber are preferred. Dessert wines such as Sauternes go into white, sherries into brown bottles. Champagnes into flagon size heavy bottles.

A full size wine bottle holds 26⅔ oz. i.e. ⅛ gallon; a half size holds 13 oz. or $\frac{1}{12}$ gallon.

Magnum	2 bottles = ⅓ gallon
Jeroboam	4 bottles (a double magnum)
Rehoboam	6 bottles = 1 gallon
Methuselah	8 bottles
Salmanazar	12 bottles = 2 gallon
Balthazar	16 bottles
Nebuchadnezzar	20 bottles

BOTTOMS: the same as lees, the deposit in a fermenter or storage vessel.

BOUQUET: the aroma of a wine.

BRANDY: an alcoholic beverage distilled from wine.

CARBON DIOXIDE: the gas which is evolved during fermentation.

CARBONATED WINES: wines rendered sparkling by injecting carbon dioxide gas into still wines.

CASKS: these are oak containers of various sizes as follows.

A Fuder of German wine approx.	220 gallons
A tonneau or tun of burgundy	190 gallons
Pipe of port	115 gallons
Butt of sherry	108 gallons
Hogshead of port	57 gallons
Hogshead of sherry	54 gallons

CASKS (BEER):

Barrel	36 gallons
Kilderkin	18 gallons
Firkin	9 gallons
Pin	4½ gallons

CREAM OF TARTAR: the white crystalline deposit which settles out from grape wines during cold weather or chilling.

CRIADERA: successive stages in blending sherries.

FERMENTATION: the process due to yeast activity which converts a sugary fluid into one containing alcohol, i.e. a fruit juice into wine.

Primary fermentation—the first vigorous fermentation.

Secondary fermentation—a subsequent slower fermentation.

FINING: a method of clarifying a wine by adding to it an inert or a soluble substance which becomes insoluble by interaction with tannin and settles down to the bottom, pulling suspended matter down with it.

FINO: a dry light sherry matured under Flor.

FLOWERS OF WINE: a white skin which gradually forms on wines exposed to air. This will decompose the wine eventually. (Not to be confused with Flor, a sherry film.)

FLOR: sherry yeast under some conditions will form a wrinkled skin consisting of yeast on top of sherry causing it to develop strong sherry flavour and to become dry and pale.

FORTIFICATION: the addition of grape spirit or other strong alcohol to wine or grape juice as in the production of sherry and port.

GALLON: 8 pints or 160 oz. make one Imperial gallon. The American gallon is only 128 oz.

MALO-LACTIC FERMENTATION: see under Acid.

OENOLOGY: study of wine—also spelt Enology.

OENOLOGIST: student of wine—also spelt Enologist.

OLOROSO: a sweet full bodied dark sherry.

OXIDATION: browning under the influence of air which causes spoilage except in the case of sherry which is an oxidised wine.

PETILLANT: a wine which has a slight content of carbon dioxide.

RACKING: drawing or syphoning off a clear wine from the deposit.

SOLERA: a system of maturing and blending sherry.

SPARKLING WINE: a wine retaining natural effervescence such as champagne.

VINIFICATION: the conversion into wine of any juice but mainly grape juice.

VINTAGE: the harvesting of the grapes.

VINTNER: wine maker.

VITICULTURIST: vine grower.

INDEX